THE LIFE

THY KINGDOM COME

Biblica offers a range of biblical resources priced for ministry.
Please contact us for more information.

Biblica Europe

Website: BiblicaEurope.com
E-mail: BiblicaEurope@Biblica.com
Phone: 02890 735 875
Mail: The Mount, 2 Woodstock Link, Belfast, BT6 8DD

Biblica provides God's Word to people through Bible translation & publishing, and Bible engagement in Africa, Asia Pacific, Europe, Latin America, Middle East, North America, and South Asia. Through its worldwide reach, Biblica engages people with God's Word so that their lives are transformed through a relationship with Jesus Christ.

978-1-911574-02-6

AN ACCOUNT OF THE LIFE OF JESUS CHRIST BY LUKE

LUKE'S GOSPEL

Introduced by
The Most Revd Justin Welby,
Archbishop of Canterbury

The most important thing I've ever done is become a follower of Jesus. I took my first steps with him over 40 years ago. He's been a faithful friend, a sovereign Lord – compassionate, forgiving and my ever-present saviour. Jesus is everything in my life, the heart and foundation of all I am.

Both in the best and most joyful times in my life, and through the hardest and most painful experiences, Jesus has walked alongside me. He's never left. When I felt ready to give up hope, he picked me up and it's his love that has healed me and strengthened me.

Following Jesus has been the core point of my life. But he is not just for me: he's for everyone. The greatest desire of my life is for every person to hear his voice calling to them, and to learn what it is to find his love, his call, his direction, his purpose. The best decision anyone can ever make is to become a follower of Jesus Christ.

But this life as a follower – or disciple – of Jesus only begins with an encounter with Jesus. Every day around the world this introduction happens as men and women, children and young people hear his words and catch sight of who he is in the first-hand testimonies of his life. So, I invite you to explore what it means to follow him through the pages of one of the Gospels – Luke – an account of Jesus' life specially put together so that its readers can be sure that what they've heard about Jesus is reliable and true.

Starting at the beginning and reading all the way through is as good a way as any. Or you might like to dip in and out with me as we explore some key sections which show us what following Jesus is all about.

(As we go through, I'll use this shorthand when referring to specific passages: 'Luke 10.1-15' means Luke chapter 10, verses 1 to 15.)

Luke was a Christian, probably a doctor by profession, who decided to write the account of the life of Jesus which we know today as the third of the four Gospels. Right from the start, he takes care to explain that Jesus isn't a mythical figure made up by a story-teller but that he is real and lived at a particular point in human history. Luke 1.1-4 sets out his method of doing careful research among people who have seen for themselves who Jesus is and what he has done. And have a look at the beginning of chapters 2 and 3 to see how he anchors the story of Jesus in a particular time and place. The important thing is that the Jesus we're being invited to follow is firmly located as a real figure in human history.

It isn't just that he lived, it is who he is. But what is it that makes him so special? What makes him worth following?

Luke begins by setting the scene and telling us about the circumstances surrounding the beginning of Jesus' life. We meet a number of people in the story, each of whom has a particular part to play in shedding light on the identity and significance of Jesus. There's John, a kind of 'warm-up act' to prepare the way for Jesus by drawing attention to what a remarkable person he is. John is introduced in Luke 1.5-25 and pops up at several key points until King Herod has him put to death near the start of chapter 9. Then there's the story of Mary's pregnancy and Jesus' birth – with God's messenger announcing that this new baby "will be called the Son of God" (Luke 1.35). And then there are all the accounts of what

Jesus says and does once he gets going in the public arena. It all begins on day one with an incident recorded in Luke 3.21-23 when Jesus' own understanding of who he is receives affirmation from God in a dramatic and powerful experience.

Much of what Luke writes is to help his readers come to a view about the angel's message at the start – "a Saviour has been born to you. He is the Messiah, the Lord" (Luke 2.12). Could going along with this be the best way of explaining this wonderful and extraordinary person? This is the conclusion that Luke invites us to come to. To take just one example, have a look at the incident recorded in Luke 5.17-26, with its key description of Jesus as 'Son of Man' (a technical term which means, in effect, 'Son of God'). As you read what Luke has to say, what conclusions do you begin to come to? To follow Jesus is to begin a journey of recognising who he is.

FOLLOWING JESUS IS ABOUT HEARING AND RESPONDING TO HIS CALL

Luke describes what happened when Jesus began to invite people to join him in Luke 5.1-11. It's a great story which tells us a lot about the sort of person Jesus is. What an adventure it is to get to know and follow him!

For a start, there's his wonderful generosity. In return for Simon lending him his boat to use as a kind of floating pulpit, Jesus fixes things so that he can catch a large number of fish – so many, in fact, that the nets can't cope and begin to break! I like the fact that this miracle isn't simply a spectacular stunt which Jesus pulls off all by himself. It needs Simon to do his bit as well – letting down his nets for a catch – even though, as Luke tells us, he thinks it will be a complete waste of time. But the natural authority of Jesus leads him to do it anyway, albeit a bit grudgingly. There are echoes here for us as Jesus enables Simon – tired as he is from working fruitlessly all night – to step beyond what his experience leads him to expect and tap into something fresh and exciting.

The result is that, together with James and John, Simon decides to leave everything behind and begin to follow Jesus. The three of them become active members of 'Team Jesus', going around with him and sharing in his work of changing the world one person at a time by inviting them to follow Jesus.

It's a work that is still going on today. All over the world, the lives of ordinary people are being transformed as they become captivated by Jesus and drawn into the family of those who have committed their lives to him. Simon was one of the first to follow Jesus – but he certainly wasn't the last! To follow Jesus is to join a long line of people from all over the world and throughout the last 2,000 years of history who have heard and responded to his call.

FOLLOWING JESUS IS ABOUT CHANGING FOR THE BETTER

What can we expect if we decide to begin to follow Jesus? How might our lives change? To begin to answer this, let's take a look at Luke 19.1-10.

Apart from Jesus' immediate followers, Zacchaeus is one of the few people who Luke chooses to name in his Gospel. He is a wonderful example of someone whose life is completely turned around as a result of his encounter with Jesus. And the great thing is that he is the last person you would expect this to happen to!

Reading between the lines, it looks as though his job as a chief tax collector has enabled him to amass a small fortune. But there's a downside – he is an unimpressive and unpopular figure, widely regarded as a 'sinner' by the population at large (verse 7). He really isn't the sort of person you'd expect God to be interested in – so it's little wonder that people are so shocked when Jesus chooses to reach out to him.

But it turns out that finding those who are lost is something that Jesus is really keen on. Actually, he does more than 'find' them – Luke tells us that he sees his role as coming to 'save' them too. What this means is spelt out at the end of the passage where Jesus tells Zacchaeus that "Today salvation has come to your house." The proof of this is in the amazing way Zacchaeus turns his life around. And we can't help noticing that it's how Jesus treats him which is the key to unlocking the shackles of the past and setting him free. Zacchaeus begins to display the hallmarks of what a 'saved' life looks like – not least by demonstrating a passionate commitment to sort out what's gone wrong and by being extravagantly generous in the way he puts things right.

It won't be exactly the same for us, of course. But the principles are the same. A growing awareness of how special we are to Jesus, no matter how undeserving we might feel we are. And a growing desire to respond to his love by opening up our lives so that they can reflect that love to others.

I first had a clear sense of Jesus breaking into my life in October 1975. In many ways, things went on as they had before. But there was a new and abundant presence in my life that was completely and totally transformative so that I was no longer the person I had been. The world was a different place because it was suffused with the life-giving presence of Jesus. I have found that to follow Jesus is to change for the better.

Have a look at Luke 24.13-35. Two of Jesus' followers are walking back from Jerusalem to their home in a village called Emmaus. It's just a day or two after they've had to watch Jesus, the one on whom they had pinned their hopes, being put to death – publicly, cruelly, horribly. They need to try and come to terms with what has happened and so they're talking things through with one another.

And then they're joined by a stranger – an ignorant stranger, it turns out, who seems to know nothing about the momentous events that have been engulfing Jerusalem over the last few days. They tell him what they've been talking about and then the stranger brings the Bible alive to them and makes them feel they're really connecting with God as he "explained to them what was said about himself in all the Scriptures" (verse 27).

As they reach their home, they invite the one we know to be Jesus – to them still a stranger – to join them. And then, at last, they recognise him – as they explain later, it was "when he broke the bread" (verse 35). Was there some characteristic way in which Jesus did this? Did they perhaps catch sight of the scars on his hands? Is that how they recognised him? We don't know. But we do know that they immediately go back to Jerusalem so that they can tell the others what has happened. The Jesus whom they had thought was gone for good is very much alive. There's the breaking of bread. And then the other thing which should perhaps have given the game away – the excitement they felt as Jesus explained what the Scriptures were about, especially in relation to himself.

I've often wondered what it must have been like to have lived back at the start of the first century and to have met Jesus during his time on earth. Would that have made it easier to follow him? Or would it have been more difficult? After all, there's no sense that people felt compelled to follow him and many chose not to, even after meeting him face to face.

Either way, one of the encouraging things for us about the account of the two disciples on the road to Emmaus is the fact that they couldn't see Jesus either. He was there – but they had no idea who he was. The parallels aren't exact – but I find that it's when I meet with others to share our journey of faith that I sense him drawing alongside us. And my experience is that carefully reading and reflecting on passages from the Bible day to day is one of the main ways in which Jesus makes himself more real to me. I know that he is alongside me, just as he was with these two on the road to Emmaus. Following Jesus is about getting to know him and this is possible even though we can't actually see him.

FOLLOWING JESUS IS NOT ABOUT BECOMING MORE RELIGIOUS

We encounter something that becomes a big problem for Jesus and his followers in Luke 6.1-11. And it comes from a rather surprising source. You might have thought that people who already have God on their agenda will be on side with someone like Jesus. But although that can often be the case – take the wonderful story of Simeon and Anna in Luke 2.40-52, for example – it isn't necessarily so…

Out of a genuine desire to help people live in ways that please God, some of the religious leaders in Jesus' day are insisting that people follow a complex web of rules and regulations. A number of these have to do with keeping one day of the week as a day of rest. No work is allowed on the Sabbath – not even anything that looks okay to start with but which could all too easily drift into becoming work. That's what's going on here as the disciples "began to break off some ears of corn, rubbed them in their hands and ate them."

For the religious leaders, this is completely unacceptable. Why is Jesus, who is supposed to know a thing or two about God, letting his followers get away with such a flagrant breach of God's law? But Jesus is having none of it. God's rules are really important – but their purpose is to help us flourish, not to make our lives more difficult! As he explains the next time this issue comes up in verses 6-11, what matters is that we do what we can to make things better for people, not worse.

Luke reports several situations where Jesus confronts the reality of evil and there's a vivid example of this in Luke 8.26-39. But it's striking that most of the opposition Jesus receives is from religious people, from those who have everything in place in terms of outward show but who are missing out on the inner reality. And it's what's going on inside that really matters – there's a lot more to following Jesus than simply becoming more religious.

FOLLOWING JESUS IS ABOUT BREAKING DOWN BARRIERS

Being a tax official is, of course, an entirely benign occupation these days. But as we noticed earlier when thinking about Zacchaeus, the situation was very different in Jesus' day. Tax collectors were in trouble on two fronts. In the first place, they were seen as collaborating with the occupying Roman authorities. And then, secondly, they had a nasty habit of demanding more tax than they needed to pay the Romans and pocketing the difference for themselves. So, have a look at Luke 5.27-32, where Luke introduces us to a tax collector called Levi (also known as Matthew). The encounter between him and Jesus must have been striking. Had they met before? What was it that led Levi to get up from behind his desk and leave everything in order to follow Jesus? Whatever it was, the outcome is wonderful. Levi opens up his home and invites everyone along for a great party.

Some of the religious leaders we have met before come along for the ride. They're in the mood to complain… Why isn't Jesus more careful about the company he keeps? Doesn't he know what kind of people these tax collectors and sinners are? The answer is that he does – and that's the whole point. As Jesus explains, "Healthy people don't need a doctor. Ill people do. I have not come to get those who think they are right with God to follow me. I have come to get sinners to turn away from their sins." Precisely. We're never to think of ourselves as outside the scope of those who are welcome to join God's great party. Everyone is welcome. And it works the other way round too. We're never to think of others as beyond the pale either. To follow Jesus is to copy him, not least in our attitude to other people. Barriers need to be broken down and replaced with bridges.

A recurring theme in Luke's Gospel is the subject of the suffering, death and resurrection of Jesus. There are hints in the stories surrounding his birth but it becomes explicit in passages such as Luke 9.18-27. Jesus has been asking who people think he is. Peter hits the nail on the head by saying that Jesus is "God's Messiah", the great rescue figure people were expecting God to send to put things right in the world.

This is fine as far as it goes – but how exactly is Jesus the Messiah planning to go about his rescue mission? Here's how he puts it in verse 22: "The Son of Man must suffer many things. The elders will not accept him. The chief priests and the teachers of the law will not accept him either. He must be killed and on the third day rise from the dead." We have to wait almost until the very end of the Gospel to discover the connection between this and the good news of the Christian message. Here's Luke 24.46-48: "...The Messiah will suffer. He will rise from the dead on the third day. His followers will preach in his name. They will tell others to turn away from their sins and be forgiven. People from every nation will hear it, beginning at Jerusalem. You have seen these things with your own eyes..."

And so those who decide they want to follow Jesus "must say no to themselves" (Luke 9.23) – just as he has said no to himself. This is the cost. This is what it involves.

One of the saddest incidents in the Gospel is recorded in Luke 18.18-34. A wealthy individual approaches Jesus to check that he is pressing all the right buttons in his quest to receive eternal life. But he gets more than he bargains for as Jesus goes well beyond the conventional answers he is expecting. We're dealing with an undoubtedly good man here. There is no good reason to doubt his claim to have obeyed all the commandments since he was a boy – including, presumably, the one against lying!

But here's what Jesus tells him in verse 22: "You are still missing one thing. Sell everything you have. Give the money to those who are poor. You will have treasure in heaven. Then come and follow me." In the short term at least, this is too much for him. Luke tells us that "he became very sad" and then adds, by way of explanation, that "he was very rich".

This is perhaps the starkest of the references we find in Luke's Gospel about the cost of following Jesus. There are good reasons for thinking that this particular young man is a special case and that the requirement to sell everything doesn't apply to everyone. But the rest of us can't ignore the issue altogether. Jesus talks about this when speaking to a large crowd of people back in Luke 14.25-35, where the condition of becoming one of his disciples is that "you must give up everything you have". The message is that there is only room for one at the top. In order to start following Jesus we need to stop following anyone or anything else, including ourselves. That's why those who want to follow Jesus must sit light to their wealth and possessions – which is, of course, that much harder for those who are rich.

This modern version of a prayer by John Wesley puts it rather well: "I am no longer my own, but yours. Put me to what you will, rank me with whom you will; put me to doing, put me to suffering; let me be employed for you, or laid aside for you, exalted for you, or brought low for you; let me be full, let me be empty, let me have all things, let me have nothing: I freely and wholeheartedly yield all things to your pleasure and disposal…" Following Jesus means saying 'yes' to him and 'no' to ourselves – and that is a costly thing to do.

We first met Peter when he was known as Simon, right near the beginning of the Gospel – the fisherman who was called by Jesus to stop catching fish and start catching people for God's kingdom instead. Now have a look at Luke 22.24-34. Here we see him making the confident promise to follow Jesus to the bitter end, even if to do so means being sent to prison or put to death. Brave words indeed!

What actually happens is set out in Luke 22.54-62. When it comes down to it, Peter turns out to be a disappointment. Not to Jesus – who had known exactly what would happen all along. No, Peter is above all a disappointment to himself. It's little wonder that "he broke down and cried" (verse 62) in the wake of his threefold denial that he knew Jesus.

And yet it is all sorted out and he is given a fresh start. We see him as one of the first of those who verifies that Jesus has risen from the dead in Luke 24. And when Luke comes to write his second volume, the Acts of the Apostles, which describes what the early Christians got up to after Jesus had risen from the dead and returned to heaven, it's Peter who takes the lead and becomes a powerful spokesperson for the young Christian community. He stumbles, yes, but the good news is that those who follow Jesus aren't expected to get it right all the time. He will help them get up and start again when they fail.

Let's take a final look at one of the many stories Jesus told – the 'Story of the Great Banquet', set out in Luke 14.15-24. Like several of Jesus' stories, it describes our final destination in terms of the joy and celebration of a party. This is where Jesus is leading those who follow him.

The setting for this story is itself a party where Jesus responds to a rather pious remark from one of his fellow guests: "Blessed is the one who will eat at the feast in God's kingdom" (verse 15). Jesus agrees that God's party at the end of time will indeed be the most wonderful celebration imaginable – but then challenges some assumptions about who will be there. In the vivid way he tells the story Jesus paints with broad brush strokes in order to make the point – the sobering truth is that "not one of those people who were invited will get a taste of my banquet" (verse 24).

That's bad news for those who have allowed themselves to become preoccupied with other things and let the invitation gather dust on the mantelpiece. But it's enormously good news for everyone else! We notice that the new invitations go first to those on the margins – the poor, and those who can't see or walk. They're at the front of the queue. But then there's still room. So the invitation is broadened to include anyone and everyone: "Go out to the roads. Go out to the country lanes. Make the people come in. I want my house to be full" (verse 23).

This is, remember, a story and we shouldn't press the details too far. But it does underline the wonderful generosity of a God whose doors are open to everyone. And the role of the servants in this story reminds us that inviting others to discover Jesus for themselves and get ready for the party is still a key part of what it means to follow him. He calls us to extend our hands and our hearts, use our words and lives to echo his call to every person to follow him. For the best decision anyone can ever make is to be a follower of Jesus Christ.

GOING ON FROM HERE

Would you like to take things further and explore more about how to follow Jesus? As a starting point, I suggest talking to a Christian friend – perhaps the person who gave you this Gospel – and asking them to tell their story. And do make use of your local church as a place where people gather to share together in the journey of faith. You're welcome to contact my team here at Lambeth Palace by emailing **talkaboutjesus@lambethpalace.org** and there are also some good websites which you might find useful – try **www.rejesus.org.uk** and **www.christianity.org.uk** for starters.

As a Christian it is my deepest conviction that Jesus Christ is good news – indeed the best news ever – and that following him is the best possible way to live. And so I pray for you and wish you well as you continue on the journey of discovering God's love and his grace, his forgiveness and his mercy, his grace and his faithfulness, poured out so generously and freely through Jesus Christ.

Thanks be to you, my Lord Jesus Christ,
for all the benefits you have given me,
for all the pains and insults you have borne for me.
O most merciful Redeemer, friend and brother,
may I know you more clearly,
love you more dearly,
and follow you more nearly,
day by day.   based on a prayer by St Richard of Chichester (1197-1253)

LUKE

Luke Writes an Orderly Report

1 Many people have attempted to write about the things that have taken place among us. ² Reports of these things were handed down to us. There were people who saw these things for themselves from the beginning. They saw them and then passed the word on. ³ With this in mind, I myself have carefully looked into everything from the beginning. So I also decided to write down an orderly report of exactly what happened. I am doing this for you, most excellent Theophilus. ⁴ I want you to know that the things you have been taught are true.

The Coming Birth of John the Baptist

⁵ Herod was king of Judea. During the time he was ruling, there was a priest named Zechariah. He belonged to a group of priests named after Abijah. His wife Elizabeth also came from the family line of Aaron. ⁶ Both of them did what was right in the sight of God. They obeyed all the Lord's commands and rules faithfully. ⁷ But they had no children, because Elizabeth was not able to have any. And they were both very old.

⁸ One day Zechariah's group was on duty. He was serving as a priest in God's temple. ⁹ He happened to be chosen, in the usual way, to go into the temple of the Lord. There he was supposed to burn incense. ¹⁰ The time came for this to be done. All who had gathered to worship were praying outside.

¹¹ Then an angel of the Lord appeared to Zechariah. The angel was standing at the right side of the incense altar. ¹² When Zechariah saw him, he was amazed and terrified. ¹³ But the angel said to him, "Do not be afraid, Zechariah. Your prayer has been heard. Your wife Elizabeth will have a child. It will be a boy, and you must call him John. ¹⁴ He will be a joy and delight to you. His birth will make many people very glad. ¹⁵ He will be important in the sight of the Lord. "He must never drink wine or other such drinks. He will be filled with the Holy Spirit even before he is born. ¹⁶ He will bring back many of the people of Israel to the

Lord their God. ¹⁷ And he will prepare the way for the Lord. He will have the same spirit and power that Elijah had. He will bring peace between parents and their children. He will teach people who don't obey to be wise and do what is right. In this way, he will prepare a people who are ready for the Lord."

¹⁸ Zechariah asked the angel, "How can I be sure of this? I am an old man, and my wife is old too."

¹⁹ The angel said to him, "I am Gabriel. I serve God. I have been sent to speak to you and to tell you this good news. ²⁰ And now you will have to be silent. You will not be able to speak until after John is born. That's because you did not believe my words. They will come true at the time God has chosen."

²¹ During that time, the people were waiting for Zechariah to come out of the temple. They wondered why he stayed there so long. ²² When he came out, he could not speak to them. They realised he had seen a vision in the temple. They knew this because he kept gesturing to them. He still could not speak.

²³ When his time of service was over, he returned home. ²⁴ After that, his wife Elizabeth became pregnant. She stayed at home for five months. ²⁵ "The Lord has done this for me," she said. "In these days, he has been kind to me. He has taken away my shame among the people."

The Coming Birth of Jesus

²⁶ In the sixth month after Elizabeth had become pregnant, God sent the angel Gabriel to Nazareth, a town in Galilee. ²⁷ He was sent to a virgin. The girl was engaged to a man named Joseph. He came from the family line of David. The virgin's name was Mary. ²⁸ The angel greeted her and said, "The Lord has blessed you in a special way. He is with you."

²⁹ Mary was very upset because of his words. She wondered what kind of greeting this could be. ³⁰ But the angel said to her, "Do not be afraid, Mary. God is very pleased with you. ³¹ You will become pregnant and give birth to a son. You must call him Jesus. ³² He will be great and will be called the Son of the Most High God. The Lord God will make him a king like his father David of long ago. ³³ The Son of the Most High God will rule for

ever over his people. They are from the family line of Jacob. That kingdom will never end."

³⁴ "How can this happen?" Mary asked the angel. "I am a virgin."

³⁵ The angel answered, "The Holy Spirit will come to you. The power of the Most High God will cover you. So the holy one that is born will be called the Son of God. ³⁶ Your relative Elizabeth will have a child even though she is old. People thought she could not have children. But she has been pregnant for six months now. ³⁷ That's because what God says will always come true."

³⁸ "I serve the Lord," Mary answered. "May it happen to me just as you said it would." Then the angel left her.

Mary Visits Elizabeth

³⁹ At that time Mary got ready and hurried to a town in Judea's hill country. ⁴⁰ There she entered Zechariah's home and greeted Elizabeth. ⁴¹ When Elizabeth heard Mary's greeting, the baby inside her jumped. And Elizabeth was filled with the Holy Spirit. ⁴² In a loud voice she called out, "God has blessed you more than other women. And blessed is the child you will have! ⁴³ But why is God so kind to me? Why has the mother of my Lord come to me? ⁴⁴ As soon as I heard the sound of your voice, the baby inside me jumped for joy. ⁴⁵ You are a woman God has blessed. You have believed that the Lord would keep his promises to you!"

Mary's Song

⁴⁶ Mary said,

"My soul gives glory to the Lord.
⁴⁷   My spirit delights in God my Saviour.
⁴⁸ He has taken note of me
      even though I am not considered important.
   From now on all people will call me blessed.
⁴⁹   The Mighty One has done great things for me.
      His name is holy.
⁵⁰ He shows his mercy to those who have respect for him,
      from parent to child down through the years.
⁵¹ He has done mighty things with his powerful arm.

He has scattered those who are proud in their deepest
thoughts.
⁵² He has brought down rulers from their thrones.
But he has lifted up people who are not considered
important.
⁵³ He has filled with good things those who are hungry.
But he has sent away empty those who are rich.
⁵⁴ He has helped the people of Israel, who serve him.
He has always remembered to be kind
⁵⁵ to Abraham and his children down through the years.
He has done it just as he promised to our people of
long ago."

⁵⁶ Mary stayed with Elizabeth about three months. Then she returned home.

John the Baptist Is Born

⁵⁷ The time came for Elizabeth to have her baby. She gave birth to a son. ⁵⁸ Her neighbours and relatives heard that the Lord had been very kind to her. They shared her joy.

⁵⁹ On the eighth day, they came to have the child circumcised. They were going to name him Zechariah, like his father. ⁶⁰ But his mother spoke up. "No!" she said. "He must be called John."

⁶¹ They said to her, "No-one among your relatives has that name."

⁶² Then they motioned to his father. They wanted to find out what he would like to name the child. ⁶³ He asked for something to write on. Then he wrote, "His name is John." Everyone was amazed. ⁶⁴ Right away Zechariah could speak again. Right away he praised God. ⁶⁵ All his neighbours were filled with fear and wonder. Throughout Judea's hill country, people were talking about all these things. ⁶⁶ Everyone who heard this wondered about it. And because the Lord was with John, they asked, "What is this child going to be?"

Zechariah's Song

⁶⁷ John's father Zechariah was filled with the Holy Spirit. He prophesied,

⁶⁸ "Give praise to the Lord, the God of Israel!
    He has come to his people and purchased their freedom.
⁶⁹ He has acted with great power and has saved us.
    He did it for those who are from the family line of his
        servant David.
⁷⁰ Long ago holy prophets said he would do it.
⁷¹ He has saved us from our enemies.
    We are rescued from all who hate us.
⁷² He has been kind to our people of long ago.
    He has remembered his holy covenant.
⁷³   He made a promise to our father Abraham.
⁷⁴ He promised to save us from our enemies.
    Then we could serve him without fear.
⁷⁵   He wants us to be holy and godly as long as we live.

⁷⁶ "And you, my child, will be called a prophet of the Most
        High God.
    You will go ahead of the Lord to prepare the way for him.
⁷⁷ You will tell his people how they can be saved.
    You will tell them that their sins can be forgiven.
⁷⁸ All of that will happen because our God is tender and caring.
    His kindness will bring the rising sun to us from heaven.
⁷⁹ It will shine on those living in darkness
    and in the shadow of death.
It will guide our feet on the path of peace."

⁸⁰ The child grew up, and his spirit became strong. He lived in
the desert until he appeared openly to Israel.

Jesus Is Born

2 In those days, Caesar Augustus made a law. It required that a
list be made of everyone in the whole Roman world. ² It was
the first time a list was made of the people while Quirinius was
governor of Syria. ³ Everyone went to their own town to be listed.
    ⁴ So Joseph went also. He went from the town of Nazareth in
Galilee to Judea. That is where Bethlehem, the town of David,
was. Joseph went there because he belonged to the family line
of David. ⁵ He went there with Mary to be listed. Mary was
engaged to him. She was expecting a baby. ⁶ While Joseph and

Mary were there, the time came for the child to be born. ⁷ She gave birth to her first baby. It was a boy. She wrapped him in large strips of cloth. Then she placed him in a manger. That's because there was no guest room where they could stay.

⁸ There were shepherds living out in the fields nearby. It was night, and they were taking care of their sheep. ⁹ An angel of the Lord appeared to them. And the glory of the Lord shone around them. They were terrified. ¹⁰ But the angel said to them, "Do not be afraid. I bring you good news. It will bring great joy for all the people. ¹¹ Today in the town of David a Saviour has been born to you. He is the Messiah, the Lord. ¹² Here is how you will know I am telling you the truth. You will find a baby wrapped in strips of cloth and lying in a manger."

¹³ Suddenly a large group of angels from heaven also appeared. They were praising God. They said,

¹⁴ "May glory be given to God in the highest heaven!
    And may peace be given to those he is pleased with
        on earth!"

¹⁵ The angels left and went into heaven. Then the shepherds said to one another, "Let's go to Bethlehem. Let's see this thing that has happened, which the Lord has told us about."

¹⁶ So they hurried off and found Mary and Joseph and the baby. The baby was lying in the manger. ¹⁷ After the shepherds had seen him, they told everyone. They reported what the angel had said about this child. ¹⁸ All who heard it were amazed at what the shepherds said to them. ¹⁹ But Mary kept all these things like a secret treasure in her heart. She thought about them over and over. ²⁰ The shepherds returned. They gave glory and praise to God. Everything they had seen and heard was just as they had been told.

²¹ When the child was eight days old, he was circumcised. At the same time he was named Jesus. This was the name the angel had given him before his mother became pregnant.

Joseph and Mary Take Jesus to the Temple

²² The time came for making Mary "clean" as required by the Law of Moses. So Joseph and Mary took Jesus to Jerusalem.

There they presented him to the Lord. ²³ In the Law of the Lord it says, "The first boy born in every family must be set apart for the Lord." *(Exodus 13:2,12)* ²⁴ They also offered a sacrifice. They did it in keeping with the Law, which says, "a pair of doves or two young pigeons." *(Leviticus 12:8)*

²⁵ In Jerusalem there was a man named Simeon. He was a good and godly man. He was waiting for God's promise to Israel to come true. The Holy Spirit was with him. ²⁶ The Spirit had told Simeon that he would not die before he had seen the Lord's Messiah. ²⁷ The Spirit led him into the temple courtyard. Then Jesus' parents brought the child in. They came to do for him what the Law required. ²⁸ Simeon took Jesus in his arms and praised God. He said,

²⁹ "Lord, you are the King over all.
>Now let me, your servant, go in peace.
>That is what you promised.
³⁰ My eyes have seen your salvation.
³¹   You have prepared it in the sight of all nations.
³² It is a light to be given to the Gentiles.
>It will be the glory of your people Israel."

³³ The child's father and mother were amazed at what was said about him. ³⁴ Then Simeon blessed them. He said to Mary, Jesus' mother, "This child is going to cause many people in Israel to fall and to rise. God has sent him. But many will speak against him. ³⁵ The thoughts of many hearts will be known. A sword will wound your own soul too."

³⁶ There was also a prophet named Anna. She was the daughter of Penuel from the tribe of Asher. Anna was very old. After getting married, she lived with her husband seven years. ³⁷ Then she was a widow until she was 84. She never left the temple. She worshipped night and day, praying and going without food. ³⁸ Anna came up to Jesus' family at that moment. She gave thanks to God. And she spoke about the child to all who were looking forward to the time when Jerusalem would be set free.

³⁹ Joseph and Mary did everything the Law of the Lord required. Then they returned to Galilee. They went to their own

town of Nazareth. [40] And the child grew and became strong. He was very wise. He was blessed by God's grace.

The Boy Jesus at the Temple

[41] Every year Jesus' parents went to Jerusalem for the Passover Feast. [42] When Jesus was 12 years old, they went up to the feast as usual. [43] After the feast was over, his parents left to go back home. The boy Jesus stayed behind in Jerusalem. But they were not aware of it. [44] They thought he was somewhere in their group. So they travelled on for a day. Then they began to look for him among their relatives and friends. [45] They did not find him. So they went back to Jerusalem to look for him. [46] After three days they found him in the temple courtyard. He was sitting with the teachers. He was listening to them and asking them questions. [47] Everyone who heard him was amazed at how much he understood. They also were amazed at his answers. [48] When his parents saw him, they were amazed. His mother said to him, "Son, why have you treated us like this? Your father and I have been worried about you. We have been looking for you everywhere."

[49] "Why were you looking for me?" he asked. "Didn't you know I had to be in my Father's house?" [50] But they did not understand what he meant by that.

[51] Then he went back to Nazareth with them, and he obeyed them. But his mother kept all these things like a secret treasure in her heart. [52] Jesus became wiser and stronger. He also became more and more pleasing to God and to people.

John the Baptist Prepares the Way

3 Tiberius Caesar had been ruling for 15 years. Pontius Pilate was governor of Judea. Herod was the ruler of Galilee. His brother Philip was the ruler of Iturea and Traconitis. Lysanias was ruler of Abilene. [2] Annas and Caiaphas were high priests. At that time God's word came to John, son of Zechariah, in the desert. [3] He went into all the countryside around the River Jordan. There he preached that people should be baptised and turn away from their sins. Then God would forgive them. [4] Here is what is written in the book of Isaiah the prophet. It says,

"A messenger is calling out in the desert,
'Prepare the way for the Lord.
   Make straight paths for him.
⁵ Every valley will be filled in.
   Every mountain and hill will be made level.
The crooked roads will become straight.
   The rough ways will become smooth.
⁶ And all people will see God's salvation.'" *(Isaiah 40:3-5)*

⁷ John spoke to the crowds coming to be baptised by him. He said, "You are like a nest of poisonous snakes! Who warned you to escape the coming of God's anger? ⁸ Live in a way that shows you have turned away from your sins. And don't start saying to yourselves, 'Abraham is our father.' I tell you, God can raise up children for Abraham even from these stones. ⁹ The axe is already lying at the roots of the trees. All the trees that don't produce good fruit will be cut down. They will be thrown into the fire."

¹⁰ "Then what should we do?" the crowd asked.

¹¹ John answered, "Anyone who has extra clothes should share with the one who has none. And anyone who has extra food should do the same."

¹² Even tax collectors came to be baptised. "Teacher," they asked, "what should we do?"

¹³ "Don't collect any more than you are required to," John told them.

¹⁴ Then some soldiers asked him, "And what should we do?"

John replied, "Don't force people to give you money. Don't bring false charges against people. Be happy with your pay."

¹⁵ The people were waiting. They were expecting something. They were all wondering in their hearts if John might be the Messiah. ¹⁶ John answered them all, "I baptise you with water. But one who is more powerful than I am will come. I'm not good enough to untie the straps of his sandals. He will baptise you with the Holy Spirit and fire. ¹⁷ His pitchfork is in his hand to toss the straw away from his threshing floor. He will gather the wheat into his barn. But he will burn the husks with fire that can't be put out." ¹⁸ John said many other things to warn the people. He also announced the good news to them.

¹⁹ But John found fault with Herod, the ruler of Galilee,

because of his marriage to Herodias. She was the wife of Herod's brother. John also spoke strongly to Herod about all the other evil things he had done. ²⁰ So Herod locked John up in prison. Herod added this sin to all his others.

The Baptism and Family Line of Jesus

²¹ When all the people were being baptised, Jesus was baptised too. And as he was praying, heaven was opened. ²² The Holy Spirit came to rest on him in the form of a dove. A voice came from heaven. It said, "You are my Son, and I love you. I am very pleased with you."

²³ Jesus was about 30 years old when he began his special work for God and others. It was thought that he was the son of Joseph.

Joseph was the son of Heli.
²⁴ Heli was the son of Matthat.
Matthat was the son of Levi.
Levi was the son of Melki.
Melki was the son of Jannai.
Jannai was the son of Joseph.
²⁵ Joseph was the son of Mattathias.
Mattathias was the son of Amos.
Amos was the son of Nahum.
Nahum was the son of Esli.
Esli was the son of Naggai.
²⁶ Naggai was the son of Maath.
Maath was the son of Mattathias.
Mattathias was the son of Semein.
Semein was the son of Josek.
Josek was the son of Joda.
²⁷ Joda was the son of Joanan.
Joanan was the son of Rhesa.
Rhesa was the son of Zerubbabel.
Zerubbabel was the son of Shealtiel.
Shealtiel was the son of Neri.
²⁸ Neri was the son of Melki.
Melki was the son of Addi.
Addi was the son of Cosam.
Cosam was the son of Elmadam.

Elmadam was the son of Er.
²⁹ Er was the son of Joshua.
Joshua was the son of Eliezer.
Eliezer was the son of Jorim.
Jorim was the son of Matthat.
Matthat was the son of Levi.
³⁰ Levi was the son of Simeon.
Simeon was the son of Judah.
Judah was the son of Joseph.
Joseph was the son of Jonam.
Jonam was the son of Eliakim.
³¹ Eliakim was the son of Melea.
Melea was the son of Menna.
Menna was the son of Mattatha.
Mattatha was the son of Nathan.
Nathan was the son of David.
³² David was the son of Jesse.
Jesse was the son of Obed.
Obed was the son of Boaz.
Boaz was the son of Salmon.
Salmon was the son of Nahshon.
³³ Nahshon was the son of Amminadab.
Amminadab was the son of Ram.
Ram was the son of Hezron.
Hezron was the son of Perez.
Perez was the son of Judah.
³⁴ Judah was the son of Jacob.
Jacob was the son of Isaac.
Isaac was the son of Abraham.
Abraham was the son of Terah.
Terah was the son of Nahor.
³⁵ Nahor was the son of Serug.
Serug was the son of Reu.
Reu was the son of Peleg.
Peleg was the son of Eber.
Eber was the son of Shelah.
³⁶ Shelah was the son of Cainan.
Cainan was the son of Arphaxad.

Arphaxad was the son of Shem.
Shem was the son of Noah.
Noah was the son of Lamech.
³⁷ Lamech was the son of Methuselah.
Methuselah was the son of Enoch.
Enoch was the son of Jared.
Jared was the son of Mahalalel.
Mahalalel was the son of Kenan.
³⁸ Kenan was the son of Enosh.
Enosh was the son of Seth.
Seth was the son of Adam.
Adam was the son of God.

Jesus Is Tempted in the Desert

4 Jesus, full of the Holy Spirit, left the River Jordan. The Spirit led him into the desert. ² There the devil tempted him for 40 days. Jesus ate nothing during that time. At the end of the 40 days, he was hungry.

³ The devil said to him, "If you are the Son of God, tell this stone to become bread."

⁴ Jesus answered, "It is written, 'Man must not live only on bread.'" *(Deuteronomy 8:3)*

⁵ Then the devil led Jesus up to a high place. In an instant, he showed Jesus all the kingdoms of the world. ⁶ He said to Jesus, "I will give you all their authority and glory. It has been given to me, and I can give it to anyone I want to. ⁷ If you worship me, it will all be yours."

⁸ Jesus answered, "It is written, 'Worship the Lord your God. He is the only one you should serve.'" *(Deuteronomy 6:13)*

⁹ Then the devil led Jesus to Jerusalem. He had Jesus stand on the highest point of the temple. "If you are the Son of God," he said, "throw yourself down from here. ¹⁰ It is written,

" 'The Lord will command his angels to take good care of you.
¹¹ They will lift you up in their hands.
    Then you won't trip over a stone.'" *(Psalm 91:11,12)*

¹² Jesus answered, "Scripture says, 'Do not test the Lord your God.'" *(Deuteronomy 6:16)*

¹³ When the devil finished all this tempting, he left Jesus until a better time.

Jesus Is Not Accepted in Nazareth

¹⁴ Jesus returned to Galilee in the power of the Holy Spirit. News about him spread through the whole countryside. ¹⁵ He was teaching in their synagogues, and everyone praised him.

¹⁶ Jesus went to Nazareth, where he had been brought up. On the Sabbath day he went into the synagogue as he usually did. He stood up to read. ¹⁷ And the scroll of Isaiah the prophet was handed to him. Jesus unrolled it and found the right place. There it is written,

¹⁸ "The Spirit of the Lord is on me.
  He has anointed me
  to announce the good news to poor people.
He has sent me to announce freedom for prisoners.
  He has sent me so that the blind will see again.
He wants me to set free those who are treated badly.
¹⁹   And he has sent me to announce the year when he will
      set his people free."   *(Isaiah 61:1,2)*

²⁰ Then Jesus rolled up the scroll. He gave it back to the attendant and sat down. The eyes of everyone in the synagogue were staring at him. ²¹ He began by saying to them, "Today this passage of Scripture is coming true as you listen."

²² Everyone said good things about him. They were amazed at the gracious words they heard from his lips. "Isn't this Joseph's son?" they asked.

²³ Jesus said, "Here is a saying you will certainly apply to me. 'Doctor, heal yourself!' And you will tell me this. 'Do the things here in your home town that we heard you did in Capernaum.'"

²⁴ "What I'm about to tell you is true," he continued. "A prophet is not accepted in his home town. ²⁵ I tell you for sure that there were many widows in Israel in the days of Elijah. And there had been no rain for three and a half years. There wasn't enough food to eat anywhere in the land. ²⁶ But Elijah was not sent to any of those widows. Instead, he was sent to a widow in Zarephath near Sidon. ²⁷ And there were many in Israel who had

skin diseases in the days of Elisha the prophet. But not one of them was healed except Naaman the Syrian."

²⁸ All the people in the synagogue were very angry when they heard that. ²⁹ They got up and ran Jesus out of town. They took him to the edge of the hill on which the town was built. They planned to throw him off the cliff. ³⁰ But Jesus walked right through the crowd and went on his way.

Jesus Drives Out an Evil Spirit

³¹ Then Jesus went to Capernaum, a town in Galilee. On the Sabbath day he taught the people. ³² They were amazed at his teaching, because his words had authority.

³³ In the synagogue there was a man controlled by a demon, an evil spirit. He cried out at the top of his voice. ³⁴ "Go away!" he said. "What do you want with us, Jesus of Nazareth? Have you come to destroy us? I know who you are. You are the Holy One of God!"

³⁵ "Be quiet!" Jesus said firmly. "Come out of him!" Then the demon threw the man down in front of everybody. And it came out without hurting him.

³⁶ All the people were amazed. They said to each other, "What he says is amazing! With authority and power he gives orders to evil spirits. And they come out!" ³⁷ The news about Jesus spread throughout the whole area.

Jesus Heals Many People

³⁸ Jesus left the synagogue and went to the home of Simon. At that time, Simon's mother in law was suffering from a high fever. So they asked Jesus to help her. ³⁹ He bent over her and commanded the fever to leave, and it left her. She got up right away and began to serve them.

⁴⁰ At sunset, people brought to Jesus all who were ill. He placed his hands on each one and healed them. ⁴¹ Also, demons came out of many people. The demons shouted, "You are the Son of God!" But he commanded them to be quiet. He would not allow them to speak, because they knew he was the Messiah.

⁴²At dawn, Jesus went out to a place where he could be by himself. The people went to look for him. When they found him, they tried to keep him from leaving them. ⁴³But he said, "I must announce the good news of God's kingdom to the other towns also. That is why I was sent." ⁴⁴And he kept on preaching in the synagogues of Judea.

Jesus Chooses His First Disciples

5 One day Jesus was standing by the Sea of Galilee. The people crowded around him and listened to the word of God. ²Jesus saw two boats at the edge of the water. They had been left there by the fishermen, who were washing their nets. ³He got into the boat that belonged to Simon. Jesus asked him to go out a little way from shore. Then he sat down in the boat and taught the people.

⁴When he finished speaking, he turned to Simon. Jesus said, "Go out into deep water. Let down the nets so you can catch some fish."

⁵Simon answered, "Master, we've worked hard all night and haven't caught anything. But because you say so, I will let down the nets."

⁶When they had done so, they caught a large number of fish. There were so many that their nets began to break. ⁷So they motioned to their partners in the other boat to come and help them. They came and filled both boats so full that they began to sink.

⁸When Simon Peter saw this, he fell at Jesus' knees. "Go away from me, Lord!" he said. "I am a sinful man!" ⁹He and everyone with him were amazed at the number of fish they had caught. ¹⁰So were James and John, the sons of Zebedee, who worked with Simon.

Then Jesus said to Simon, "Don't be afraid. From now on you will fish for people." ¹¹So they pulled their boats up on shore. Then they left everything and followed him.

Jesus Heals a Man Who Had a Skin Disease

¹²While Jesus was in one of the towns, a man came along. He had a skin disease all over his body. When he saw Jesus, the

man fell with his face to the ground. He begged him, "Lord, if you are willing to make me 'clean', you can do it."

¹³ Jesus reached out his hand and touched the man. "I am willing to do it," he said. "Be 'clean'!" Right away the disease left him.

¹⁴ Then Jesus ordered him, "Don't tell anyone. Go and show yourself to the priest. Offer the sacrifices that Moses commanded. It will be a witness to the priest and the people that you are 'clean'. "

¹⁵ But the news about Jesus spread even more. So crowds of people came to hear him. They also came to be healed of their diseases. ¹⁶ But Jesus often went away to be by himself and pray.

Jesus Forgives and Heals a Man Who Could Not Walk

¹⁷ One day Jesus was teaching. Pharisees and teachers of the law were sitting there. They had come from every village of Galilee and from Judea and Jerusalem. They heard that the Lord had given Jesus the power to heal the ill. ¹⁸ So some men came carrying a man who could not walk. He was lying on a mat. They tried to take him into the house to place him in front of Jesus. ¹⁹ They could not find a way to do this because of the crowd. So they went up on the roof. Then they lowered the man on his mat through the opening in the roof tiles. They lowered him into the middle of the crowd, right in front of Jesus.

²⁰ When Jesus saw that they had faith, he spoke to the man. He said, "Friend, your sins are forgiven."

²¹ The Pharisees and the teachers of the law began to think, "Who is this fellow who says such an evil thing? Who can forgive sins but God alone?"

²² Jesus knew what they were thinking. So he asked, "Why are you thinking these things in your hearts? ²³ Is it easier to say, 'Your sins are forgiven'? Or to say, 'Get up and walk'? ²⁴ But I want you to know that the Son of Man has authority on earth to forgive sins." So he spoke to the man who could not walk. "I tell you," he said, "get up. Take your mat and go home." ²⁵ Right away, the man stood up in front of them. He took his mat and went home praising God. ²⁶ Everyone was amazed and gave

praise to God. They were filled with wonder. They said, "We have seen unusual things today."

Jesus Chooses Levi and Eats with Sinners

²⁷ After this, Jesus left the house. He saw a tax collector sitting at the tax booth. The man's name was Levi. "Follow me," Jesus said to him. ²⁸ Levi got up, left everything and followed him.

²⁹ Then Levi gave a huge banquet for Jesus at his house. A large crowd of tax collectors and others were eating with them. ³⁰ But the Pharisees and their teachers of the law complained to Jesus' disciples. They said, "Why do you eat and drink with tax collectors and sinners?"

³¹ Jesus answered them, "Healthy people don't need a doctor. Ill people do. ³² I have not come to get those who think they are right with God to follow me. I have come to get sinners to turn away from their sins."

Jesus Is Asked about Fasting

³³ Some of the people who were there said to Jesus, "John's disciples often pray and go without eating. So do the disciples of the Pharisees. But yours go on eating and drinking."

³⁴ Jesus answered, "Can you make the friends of the groom fast while he is with them? ³⁵ But the time will come when the groom will be taken away from them. In those days they will go without eating."

³⁶ Then Jesus gave them an example. He said, "No-one tears a piece out of new clothes to patch old clothes. Otherwise, they will tear the new clothes. Also, the patch from the new clothes will not match the old clothes. ³⁷ No-one pours new wine into old wineskins. Otherwise, the new wine will burst the skins. The wine will run out, and the wineskins will be destroyed. ³⁸ No, new wine must be poured into new wineskins. ³⁹ After drinking old wine, no-one wants the new. They say, 'The old wine is better.'"

Jesus Is Lord of the Sabbath Day

6 One Sabbath day Jesus was walking through the cornfields. His disciples began to break off some ears of corn. They

rubbed them in their hands and ate them. ²Some of the Pharisees said, "It is against the Law to do this on the Sabbath day. Why are you doing it?"

³ Jesus answered them, "Haven't you ever read about what David did? He and his men were hungry. ⁴He entered the house of God and took the holy bread. He ate the bread that only priests were allowed to eat. David also gave some to his men." ⁵Then Jesus said to them, "The Son of Man is Lord of the Sabbath day."

⁶On another Sabbath day, Jesus went into the synagogue and was teaching. A man whose right hand was weak and twisted was there. ⁷The Pharisees and the teachers of the law were trying to find fault with Jesus. So they watched him closely. They wanted to see if he would heal on the Sabbath day. ⁸But Jesus knew what they were thinking. He spoke to the man who had the weak and twisted hand. "Get up and stand in front of everyone," he said. So the man got up and stood there.

⁹Then Jesus said to them, "What does the Law say we should do on the Sabbath day? Should we do good? Or should we do evil? Should we save life? Or should we destroy it?"

¹⁰He looked around at all of them. Then he said to the man, "Stretch out your hand." He did, and his hand had been made as good as new. ¹¹But the Pharisees and the teachers of the law were very angry. They began to talk to one another about what they might do to Jesus.

Jesus Chooses the Twelve Apostles

¹²On one of those days, Jesus went out to a mountainside to pray. He spent the night praying to God. ¹³When morning came, he called for his disciples to come to him. He chose 12 of them and made them apostles.

¹⁴Simon, whom Jesus named Peter, and his brother Andrew
James
John
Philip
Bartholomew
¹⁵Matthew

Thomas
James, son of Alphaeus
Simon who was called the Zealot
¹⁶ Judas, son of James
and Judas Iscariot who would later hand Jesus over to
his enemies.

Jesus Gives Blessings and Warnings

¹⁷ Jesus went down the mountain with them and stood on
a level place. A large crowd of his disciples was there. A large
number of other people were there too. They came from all over
Judea, including Jerusalem. They also came from the coastland
around Tyre and Sidon. ¹⁸ They had all come to hear Jesus and
to be healed of their diseases. People who were troubled by evil
spirits were made well. ¹⁹ Everyone tried to touch Jesus. Power
was coming from him and healing them all.

²⁰ Jesus looked at his disciples. He said to them,

"Blessed are you who are needy.
   God's kingdom belongs to you.
²¹ Blessed are you who are hungry now.
   You will be satisfied.
Blessed are you who are sad now.
   You will laugh.
²² Blessed are you when people hate you,
   when they have nothing to do with you
   and say bad things about you,
   and when they treat your name as something evil.
     They do all this because you are followers of the Son
     of Man.

²³ "The prophets of long ago were treated the same way. When
these things happen to you, be glad and jump for joy. You will
receive many blessings in heaven.

²⁴ "But how terrible it will be for you who are rich!
   You have already had your easy life.
²⁵ How terrible for you who are well fed now!
   You will go hungry.

How terrible for you who laugh now!
   You will cry and be sad.
²⁶ How terrible for you when everyone says good things
      about you!
   Their people treated the false prophets the same way
      long ago.

Love Your Enemies

²⁷ "But here is what I tell you who are listening. Love your enemies. Do good to those who hate you. ²⁸ Bless those who call down curses on you. And pray for those who treat you badly. ²⁹ Suppose someone slaps you on one cheek. Let them slap you on the other cheek as well. Suppose someone takes your coat. Don't stop them from taking your shirt as well. ³⁰ Give to everyone who asks you. And if anyone takes what belongs to you, don't ask to get it back. ³¹ Do to others as you want them to do to you.

³² "Suppose you love those who love you. Should anyone praise you for that? Even sinners love those who love them. ³³ And suppose you do good to those who are good to you. Should anyone praise you for that? Even sinners do that. ³⁴ And suppose you lend money to those who can pay you back. Should anyone praise you for that? Even a sinner lends to sinners, expecting them to pay everything back. ³⁵ But love your enemies. Do good to them. Lend to them without expecting to get anything back. Then you will receive a lot in return. And you will be children of the Most High God. He is kind to people who are evil and are not thankful. ³⁶ So have mercy, just as your Father has mercy.

Be Fair When You Judge Other People

³⁷ "If you do not judge other people, then you will not be judged. If you do not find others guilty, then you will not be found guilty. Forgive, and you will be forgiven. ³⁸ Give, and it will be given to you. A good amount will be poured into your lap. It will be pressed down, shaken together, and running over. The same amount you give will be measured out to you."

[39] Jesus also gave them another example. He asked, "Can a blind person lead another blind person? Won't they both fall into a pit? [40] The student is not better than the teacher. But everyone who is completely trained will be like their teacher.

[41] "You look at the bit of sawdust in your friend's eye. But you pay no attention to the piece of wood in your own eye. [42] How can you say to your friend, 'Let me take the bit of sawdust out of your eye'? How can you say this while there is a piece of wood in your own eye? You pretender! First take the piece of wood out of your own eye. Then you will be able to see clearly to take the bit of sawdust out of your friend's eye.

A Tree and Its Fruit

[43] "A good tree doesn't bear bad fruit. And a bad tree doesn't bear good fruit. [44] You can tell each tree by the kind of fruit it bears. People do not pick figs from thorns. And they don't pick grapes from bushes. [45] A good man says good things. These come from the good that is stored up in his heart. An evil man says evil things. These come from the evil that is stored up in his heart. A person's mouth says everything that is in their heart.

The Wise and Foolish Builders

[46] "Why do you call me, 'Lord, Lord', and still don't do what I say? [47] Some people come and listen to me and do what I say. I will show you what they are like. [48] They are like a man who builds a house. He digs down deep and sets it on solid rock. When a flood comes, the river rushes against the house. But the water can't shake it. The house is well built. [49] But here is what happens when people listen to my words and do not obey them. They are like a man who builds a house on soft ground instead of solid rock. The moment the river rushes against that house, it falls down. It is completely destroyed."

A Roman Commander Has Faith

7 Jesus finished saying all these things to the people who were listening. Then he entered Capernaum. [2] There the servant of a Roman commander was ill and about to die. His master

thought highly of him. ³ The commander heard about Jesus. So he sent some elders of the Jews to him. He told them to ask Jesus to come and heal his servant. ⁴ They came to Jesus and begged him, "This man deserves to have you do this. ⁵ He loves our nation and has built our synagogue." ⁶ So Jesus went with them.

When Jesus came near the house, the Roman commander sent friends to him. He told them to say, "Lord, don't trouble yourself. I am not good enough to have you come into my house. ⁷ That is why I did not even think I was fit to come to you. But just say the word, and my servant will be healed. ⁸ I myself am a man who is under authority. And I have soldiers who obey my orders. I tell this one, 'Go', and he goes. I tell that one, 'Come', and he comes. I say to my servant, 'Do this', and he does it."

⁹ When Jesus heard this, he was amazed at the commander. Jesus turned to the crowd that was following him. He said, "I tell you, even in Israel I have not found anyone whose faith is so strong." ¹⁰ Then the men who had been sent to Jesus returned to the house. They found that the servant was healed.

Jesus Raises a Widow's Son from the Dead

¹¹ Some time later, Jesus went to a town called Nain. His disciples and a large crowd went along with him. ¹² He approached the town gate. Just then, a dead person was being carried out. He was the only son of his mother. She was a widow. A large crowd from the town was with her. ¹³ When the Lord saw her, he felt sorry for her. So he said, "Don't cry."

¹⁴ Then he went up and touched the coffin. Those carrying it stood still. Jesus said, "Young man, I say to you, get up!" ¹⁵ The dead man sat up and began to talk. Then Jesus gave him back to his mother.

¹⁶ The people were all filled with wonder and praised God. "A great prophet has appeared among us," they said. "God has come to help his people." ¹⁷ This news about Jesus spread all through Judea and the whole country.

Jesus and John the Baptist

¹⁸ John's disciples told him about all these things. So he chose two of them. ¹⁹ He sent them to the Lord. John told them to ask

him, "Are you the one who is supposed to come? Or should we look for someone else?"

²⁰ The men came to Jesus. They said, "John the Baptist sent us to ask you, 'Are you the one who is supposed to come? Or should we look for someone else?'"

²¹ At that time Jesus healed many people. They had illnesses, diseases and evil spirits. He also gave sight to many who were blind. ²² So Jesus replied to the messengers, "Go back to John. Tell him what you have seen and heard. Blind people receive sight. Disabled people walk. Those who have skin diseases are made 'clean'. Deaf people hear. Those who are dead are raised to life. And the good news is announced to those who are poor. ²³ Blessed is anyone who does not give up their faith because of me."

²⁴ So John's messengers left. Then Jesus began to speak to the crowd about John. He said, "What did you go out into the desert to see? Tall grass waving in the wind? ²⁵ If not, what did you go out to see? A man dressed in fine clothes? No. Those who wear fine clothes and have many expensive things are in palaces. ²⁶ Then what did you go out to see? A prophet? Yes, I tell you, and more than a prophet. ²⁷ He is the one written about in Scripture. It says,

" 'I will send my messenger ahead of you.
  He will prepare your way for you.'   (Malachi 3:1)

²⁸ I tell you, no-one more important than John has ever been born. But the least important person in God's kingdom is more important than John is."

²⁹ All the people who heard Jesus' words agreed that God's way was right. Even the tax collectors agreed. These people had all been baptised by John. ³⁰ But the Pharisees and the authorities on the law did not accept for themselves God's purpose. So they had not been baptised by John.

³¹ Jesus went on to say, "What can I compare today's people to? What are they like? ³² They are like children sitting in the market and calling out to each other. They say,

" 'We played the flute for you.
  But you didn't dance.

We sang a funeral song.
But you didn't cry.'

[33] "That is how it has been with John the Baptist. When he came to you, he didn't eat bread or drink wine. And you say, 'He has a demon.' [34] But when the Son of Man came, he ate and drank as you do. And you say, 'This fellow is always eating and drinking far too much. He's a friend of tax collectors and sinners.' [35] All who follow wisdom prove that wisdom is right."

A Sinful Woman Pours Perfume on Jesus

[36] One of the Pharisees invited Jesus to have dinner with him. So he went to the Pharisee's house. He took his place at the table. [37] There was a woman in that town who had lived a sinful life. She learned that Jesus was eating at the Pharisee's house. So she came there with a special jar of perfume. [38] She stood behind Jesus and cried at his feet. And she began to wet his feet with her tears. Then she wiped them with her hair. She kissed them and poured perfume on them.

[39] The Pharisee who had invited Jesus saw this. He said to himself, "If this man were a prophet, he would know who is touching him. He would know what kind of woman she is. She is a sinner!"

[40] Jesus answered him, "Simon, I have something to tell you."

"Tell me, teacher," he said.

[41] "Two people owed money to a certain lender. One owed him 500 silver coins. The other owed him 50 silver coins. [42] Neither of them had the money to pay him back. So he let them go without paying. Which of them will love him more?"

[43] Simon replied, "I suppose the one who owed the most money."

"You are right," Jesus said.

[44] Then he turned towards the woman. He said to Simon, "Do you see this woman? I came into your house. You did not give me any water to wash my feet. But she wet my feet with her tears and wiped them with her hair. [45] You did not give me a kiss. But this woman has not stopped kissing my feet since I came in. [46] You did not put any olive oil on my head. But she has poured

this perfume on my feet. ⁴⁷ So I tell you this. Her many sins have been forgiven. She has shown that she understands this by her great acts of love. But whoever who has been forgiven only a little loves only a little."

⁴⁸ Then Jesus said to her, "Your sins are forgiven."

⁴⁹ The other guests began to talk about this among themselves. They said, "Who is this who even forgives sins?"

⁵⁰ Jesus said to the woman, "Your faith has saved you. Go in peace."

The Story of the Farmer

8 After this, Jesus travelled around from one town and village to another. He announced the good news of God's kingdom. His 12 disciples were with him. ² So were some women who had been healed of evil spirits and diseases. One was Mary Magdalene. Seven demons had come out of her. ³ Another was Joanna, the wife of Chuza. He was the manager of Herod's household. Susanna and many others were there also. These women were helping to support Jesus and the 12 disciples with their own money.

⁴ A large crowd gathered together. People came to Jesus from town after town. As they did, he told a story. He said, ⁵ "A farmer went out to plant his seed. He scattered the seed on the ground. Some fell on a path. People walked on it, and the birds ate it up. ⁶ Some seed fell on rocky ground. When it grew, the plants dried up because they had no water. ⁷ Other seed fell among thorns. The thorns grew up with it and crowded out the plants. ⁸ Still other seed fell on good soil. It grew up and produced a crop 100 times more than the farmer planted."

When Jesus said this, he called out, "Whoever has ears should listen."

⁹ His disciples asked him what the story meant. ¹⁰ He said, "You have been given the chance to understand the secrets of God's kingdom. But to outsiders I speak by using stories. In that way,

" 'They see, but they will not know what they are seeing.
   They hear, but they will not understand what they
       are hearing.'   *(Isaiah 6:9)*

¹¹ "Here is what the story means. The seed is God's message. ¹² The seed on the path stands for God's message in the hearts of those who hear. But then the devil comes. He takes away the message from their hearts. He does it so they won't believe. Then they can't be saved. ¹³ The seed on rocky ground stands for those who hear the message and receive it with joy. But they have no roots. They believe for a while. But when they are tested, they fall away from the faith. ¹⁴ The seed that fell among thorns stands for those who hear the message. But as they go on their way, they are choked by life's worries, riches and pleasures. So they do not reach full growth. ¹⁵ But the seed on good soil stands for those with an honest and good heart. Those people hear the message. They keep it in their hearts. They remain faithful and produce a good crop.

A Lamp on a Stand

¹⁶ "No-one lights a lamp and then hides it in a clay jar or puts it under a bed. Instead, they put it on a stand. Then those who come in can see its light. ¹⁷ What is hidden will be seen. And what is out of sight will be brought into the open and made known. ¹⁸ So be careful how you listen. Whoever has something will be given more. Whoever has nothing, even what they think they have will be taken away from them."

Jesus' Mother and Brothers

¹⁹ Jesus' mother and brothers came to see him. But they could not get near him because of the crowd. ²⁰ Someone told him, "Your mother and brothers are standing outside. They want to see you."

²¹ He replied, "My mother and brothers are those who hear God's word and do what it says."

Jesus Calms the Storm

²² One day Jesus said to his disciples, "Let's go over to the other side of the lake." So they got into a boat and left. ²³ As they sailed, Jesus fell asleep. A storm came down on the lake.

It was so bad that the boat was about to sink. They were in great danger.

²⁴ The disciples went and woke Jesus up. They said, "Master! Master! We're going to drown!"

He got up and ordered the wind and the huge waves to stop. The storm quietened down. It was completely calm. ²⁵ "Where is your faith?" he asked his disciples.

They were amazed and full of fear. They asked one another, "Who is this? He commands even the winds and the waves, and they obey him."

Jesus Heals a Man Controlled by Demons

²⁶ Jesus and his disciples sailed to the area of the Gerasenes across the lake from Galilee. ²⁷ When Jesus stepped on shore, he was met by a man from the town. The man was controlled by demons. For a long time he had not worn clothes or lived in a house. He lived in the tombs. ²⁸ When he saw Jesus, he cried out and fell at his feet. He shouted at the top of his voice, "Jesus, Son of the Most High God, what do you want with me? I beg you, don't hurt me!" ²⁹ This was because Jesus had commanded the evil spirit to come out of the man. Many times the spirit had taken hold of him. The man's hands and feet were chained, and he was kept under guard. But he had broken his chains. And then the demon had forced him to go out into lonely places in the countryside.

³⁰ Jesus asked him, "What is your name?"

"Legion," he replied, because many demons had gone into him. ³¹ And they begged Jesus again and again not to order them to go into the Abyss.

³² A large herd of pigs was feeding there on the hillside. The demons begged Jesus to let them go into the pigs. And he allowed it. ³³ When the demons came out of the man, they went into the pigs. Then the herd rushed down the steep bank. They ran into the lake and drowned.

³⁴ Those who were tending the pigs saw what had happened. They ran off and reported it in the town and countryside. ³⁵ The people went out to see what had happened. Then they came to Jesus. They found the man who was now free of the demons. He

was sitting at Jesus' feet. He was dressed and thinking clearly. All this made the people afraid. [36] Those who had seen it told the others how the man who had been controlled by demons was now healed. [37] Then all the people who lived in the area of the Gerasenes asked Jesus to leave them. They were filled with fear. So he got into the boat and left.

[38] The man who was now free of the demons begged to go with him. But Jesus sent him away. He said to him, [39] "Return home and tell how much God has done for you." So the man went away. He told people all over town how much Jesus had done for him.

Jesus Heals a Dead Girl and a Suffering Woman

[40] When Jesus returned, a crowd welcomed him. They were all expecting him. [41] Then a man named Jairus came. He was a synagogue leader. He fell at Jesus' feet and begged Jesus to come to his house. [42] His only daughter was dying. She was about 12 years old. As Jesus was on his way, the crowds almost crushed him.

[43] A woman was there who had a sickness that made her bleed. Her sickness had lasted for 12 years. No-one could heal her. [44] She came up behind Jesus and touched the edge of his clothes. Right away her bleeding stopped.

[45] "Who touched me?" Jesus asked.

Everyone said they didn't do it. Then Peter said, "Master, the people are crowding and pushing against you."

[46] But Jesus said, "Someone touched me. I know that power has gone out from me."

[47] The woman realised that people would notice her. Shaking with fear, she came and fell at his feet. In front of everyone, she told why she had touched him. She also told how she had been healed in an instant. [48] Then he said to her, "Dear woman, your faith has healed you. Go in peace."

[49] While Jesus was still speaking, someone came from the house of Jairus. Jairus was the synagogue leader. "Your daughter is dead," the messenger said. "Don't bother the teacher anymore."

⁵⁰ Hearing this, Jesus said to Jairus, "Don't be afraid. Just believe. She will be healed."

⁵¹ When he arrived at the house of Jairus, he did not let everyone go in with him. He took only Peter, John and James, and the child's father and mother. ⁵² During this time, all the people were crying and sobbing loudly over the child. "Stop crying!" Jesus said. "She is not dead. She is sleeping."

⁵³ They laughed at him. They knew she was dead. ⁵⁴ But he took her by the hand and said, "My child, get up!" ⁵⁵ Her spirit returned, and right away she stood up. Then Jesus told them to give her something to eat. ⁵⁶ Her parents were amazed. But Jesus ordered them not to tell anyone what had happened.

Jesus Sends Out the Twelve Disciples

9 Jesus called together the 12 disciples. He gave them power and authority to drive out all demons and to heal diseases. ² Then he sent them out to announce God's kingdom and to heal those who were ill. ³ He told them, "Don't take anything for the journey. Do not take a walking stick or a bag. Do not take any bread, money or extra clothes. ⁴ When you are invited into a house, stay there until you leave town. ⁵ Some people may not welcome you. If they don't, leave their town and shake the dust off your feet. This will be a witness against the people living there." ⁶ So the 12 disciples left. They went from village to village. They announced the good news and healed people everywhere.

⁷ Now Herod, the ruler of Galilee, heard about everything that was going on. He was bewildered, because some were saying that John the Baptist had been raised from the dead. ⁸ Others were saying that Elijah had appeared. Still others were saying that a prophet of long ago had come back to life. ⁹ But Herod said, "I had John's head cut off. So who is it that I hear such things about?" And he tried to see Jesus.

Jesus Feeds the Five Thousand

¹⁰ The disciples returned. They told Jesus what they had done. Then he took them with him. They went off by themselves to a town called Bethsaida. ¹¹ But the crowds learned about it and

followed Jesus. He welcomed them and spoke to them about God's kingdom. He also healed those who needed to be healed.

[12] Late in the afternoon the 12 disciples came to him. They said, "Send the crowd away. They can go to the nearby villages and countryside. There they can find food and a place to stay. There is nothing here."

[13] Jesus replied, "You give them something to eat."

The disciples answered, "We have only five loaves of bread and two fish. We would have to go and buy food for all this crowd." [14] About 5,000 men were there.

But Jesus said to his disciples, "Have them sit down in groups of about 50 each." [15] The disciples did so, and everyone sat down. [16] Jesus took the five loaves and the two fish. He looked up to heaven and gave thanks. He broke them into pieces. Then he gave them to the disciples to give to the people. [17] All of them ate and were satisfied. The disciples picked up 12 baskets of leftover pieces.

Peter Says That Jesus Is the Messiah

[18] One day Jesus was praying alone. Only his disciples were with him. He asked them, "Who do the crowds say I am?"

[19] They replied, "Some say John the Baptist. Others say Elijah. Still others say that one of the prophets of long ago has come back to life."

[20] "But what about you?" he asked. "Who do you say I am?"

Peter answered, "God's Messiah."

Jesus Speaks about His Coming Death

[21] Jesus strongly warned them not to tell this to anyone. [22] He said, "The Son of Man must suffer many things. The elders will not accept him. The chief priests and the teachers of the law will not accept him either. He must be killed and on the third day rise from the dead."

[23] Then he said to all of them, "Whoever wants to follow me must say no to themselves. They must pick up their cross every day and follow me. [24] Whoever wants to save their life will lose it. But whoever loses their life for me will save it. [25] What good is it if someone gains the whole world but loses or gives up their very

self? ²⁶ Suppose someone is ashamed of me and my words. The Son of Man will come in his glory and in the glory of the Father and the holy angels. Then he will be ashamed of that person.

²⁷ "What I'm about to tell you is true. Some who are standing here will not die before they see God's kingdom."

Jesus' Appearance Is Changed

²⁸ About eight days after Jesus said this, he went up on a mountain to pray. He took Peter, John and James with him. ²⁹ As he was praying, the appearance of his face changed. His clothes became as bright as a flash of lightning. ³⁰ Two men, Moses and Elijah, appeared in shining glory. Jesus and the two of them talked together. ³¹ They talked about how he would be leaving them soon. This was going to happen in Jerusalem. ³² Peter and his companions had been very sleepy. But then they became completely awake. They saw Jesus' glory and the two men standing with him. ³³ As the men were leaving Jesus, Peter spoke up. "Master," he said to him, "it is good for us to be here. Let us put up three shelters. One will be for you, one for Moses, and one for Elijah." Peter didn't really know what he was saying.

³⁴ While he was speaking, a cloud appeared and covered them. The disciples were afraid as they entered the cloud. ³⁵ A voice came from the cloud. It said, "This is my Son, and I have chosen him. Listen to him." ³⁶ When the voice had spoken, they found that Jesus was alone. The disciples kept quiet about this. They didn't tell anyone at that time what they had seen.

Jesus Heals a Boy Who Is Controlled by an Evil Spirit

³⁷ The next day Jesus and those who were with him came down from the mountain. A large crowd met Jesus. ³⁸ A man in the crowd called out. "Teacher," he said, "I beg you to look at my son. He is my only child. ³⁹ A spirit takes hold of him, and he suddenly screams. It throws him into fits so that he foams at the mouth. It hardly ever leaves him. It is destroying him. ⁴⁰ I begged your disciples to drive it out. But they couldn't do it."

⁴¹ "You unbelieving and evil people!" Jesus replied. "How long do I have to stay with you? How long do I have to put up with you?" Then he said to the man, "Bring your son here."

[42] Even while the boy was coming, the demon threw him into a fit. The boy fell to the ground. But Jesus ordered the evil spirit to leave the boy. Then Jesus healed him and gave him back to his father. [43] They were all amazed at God's greatness.

Jesus Speaks a Second Time about His Coming Death

Everyone was wondering about all that Jesus did. Then Jesus said to his disciples, [44] "Listen carefully to what I am about to tell you. The Son of Man is going to be handed over to men." [45] But they didn't understand what this meant. That was because it was hidden from them. And they were afraid to ask Jesus about it.

Who Is the Most Important Person?

[46] The disciples began to argue about which one of them would be the most important person. [47] Jesus knew what they were thinking. So he took a little child and stood the child beside him. [48] Then he spoke to them. "Anyone who welcomes this little child in my name welcomes me," he said. "And anyone who welcomes me welcomes the one who sent me. The one considered least important among all of you is really the most important."

[49] "Master," said John, "we saw someone driving out demons in your name. We tried to stop him, because he is not one of us."

[50] "Do not stop him," Jesus said. "Anyone who is not against you is for you."

The Samaritans Do Not Welcome Jesus

[51] The time grew near for Jesus to be taken up to heaven. So he made up his mind to go to Jerusalem. [52] He sent messengers on ahead. They went into a Samaritan village to get things ready for him. [53] But the people there did not welcome Jesus. That was because he was heading for Jerusalem. [54] The disciples James and John saw this. They asked, "Lord, do you want us to call down fire from heaven to destroy them?" [55] But Jesus turned and commanded them not to do it. [56] Then Jesus and his disciples went on to another village.

The Cost of Following Jesus

[57] Once Jesus and those who were with him were walking along the road. A man said to Jesus, "I will follow you no matter where you go."

[58] Jesus replied, "Foxes have dens. Birds have nests. But the Son of Man has no place to lay his head."

[59] He said to another man, "Follow me."

But the man replied, "Lord, first let me go and bury my father."

[60] Jesus said to him, "Let dead people bury their own dead. You go and tell others about God's kingdom."

[61] Still another person said, "I will follow you, Lord. But first let me go back and say goodbye to my family."

[62] Jesus replied, "Suppose someone starts to plough and then looks back. That person is not fit for service in God's kingdom."

Jesus Sends Out the Seventy two

10 After this the Lord appointed 72 others. He sent them out two by two ahead of him. They went to every town and place where he was about to go. [2] He told them, "The harvest is huge, but the workers are few. So ask the Lord of the harvest to send out workers into his harvest field. [3] Go! I am sending you out like lambs among wolves. [4] Do not take a purse or bag or sandals. And don't greet anyone on the road.

[5] "When you enter a house, first say, 'May this house be blessed with peace.' [6] If someone there works to bring peace, your blessing of peace will rest on them. If not, it will return to you. [7] Stay there, and eat and drink anything they give you. Workers are worthy of their pay. Do not move around from house to house.

[8] "When you enter a town and are welcomed, eat what is given to you. [9] Heal the ill people who are there. Tell them, 'God's kingdom has come near to you.' [10] But what if you enter a town and are not welcomed? Then go into its streets and say, [11] 'We wipe from our feet even the dust of your town. We do it to warn you. But here is what you can be sure of. God's kingdom has come near.' [12] I tell you this. On judgment day it will be easier for Sodom than for that town.

¹³ "How terrible it will be for you, Chorazin! How terrible for you, Bethsaida! Suppose the miracles done in you had been done in Tyre and Sidon. They would have turned away from their sins long ago. They would have put on the rough clothing people wear when they're sad. They would have sat down in ashes. ¹⁴ On judgment day it will be easier for Tyre and Sidon than for you. ¹⁵ And what about you, Capernaum? Will you be lifted up to the heavens? No! You will go down to the place of the dead.

¹⁶ "Whoever listens to you listens to me. Whoever does not accept you does not accept me. But whoever does not accept me does not accept the one who sent me."

¹⁷ The 72 returned with joy. They said, "Lord, even the demons obey us when we speak in your name."

¹⁸ Jesus replied, "I saw Satan fall like lightning from heaven. ¹⁹ I have given you authority to walk all over snakes and scorpions. You will be able to destroy all the power of the enemy. Nothing will harm you. ²⁰ But do not be glad when the evil spirits obey you. Instead, be glad that your names are written in heaven."

²¹ At that time Jesus was full of joy through the Holy Spirit. He said, "I praise you, Father. You are Lord of heaven and earth. You have hidden these things from wise and educated people. But you have shown them to little children. Yes, Father. This is what you wanted to do.

²² "My Father has given all things to me. The Father is the only one who knows who the Son is. And the only ones who know the Father are the Son and those to whom the Son chooses to make the Father known."

²³ Then Jesus turned to his disciples. He said to them in private, "Blessed are the eyes that see what you see. ²⁴ I tell you, many prophets and kings wanted to see what you see. But they didn't see it. They wanted to hear what you hear. But they didn't hear it."

The Story of the Good Samaritan

²⁵ One day an authority on the law stood up to test Jesus. "Teacher," he asked, "what must I do to receive eternal life?"

²⁶ "What is written in the Law?" Jesus replied. "How do you understand it?"

27 He answered, " 'Love the Lord your God with all your heart and with all your soul. Love him with all your strength and with all your mind.' *(Deuteronomy 6:5)* And, 'Love your neighbour as you love yourself.' " *(Leviticus 19:18)*

28 "You have answered correctly," Jesus replied. "Do that, and you will live."

29 But the man wanted to make himself look good. So he asked Jesus, "And who is my neighbour?"

30 Jesus replied, "A man was going down from Jerusalem to Jericho. Robbers attacked him. They stripped off his clothes and beat him. Then they went away, leaving him almost dead. 31 A priest happened to be going down that same road. When he saw the man, he passed by on the other side. 32 A Levite also came by. When he saw the man, he passed by on the other side too. 33 But a Samaritan came to the place where the man was. When he saw the man, he felt sorry for him. 34 He went to him, poured olive oil and wine on his wounds and bandaged them. Then he put the man on his own donkey. He brought him to an inn and took care of him. 35 The next day he took out two silver coins. He gave them to the owner of the inn. 'Take care of him,' he said. 'When I return, I will pay you back for any extra expense you may have.'

36 "Which of the three do you think was a neighbour to the man who was attacked by robbers?"

37 The authority on the law replied, "The one who felt sorry for him."

Jesus told him, "Go and do as he did."

Jesus at the Home of Martha and Mary

38 Jesus and his disciples went on their way. Jesus came to a village where a woman named Martha lived. She welcomed him into her home. 39 She had a sister named Mary. Mary sat at the Lord's feet listening to what he said. 40 But Martha was busy with all the things that had to be done. She came to Jesus and said, "Lord, my sister has left me to do the work by myself. Don't you care? Tell her to help me!"

41 "Martha, Martha," the Lord answered. "You are worried and upset about many things. 42 But few things are needed. Really,

only one thing is needed. Mary has chosen what is better. And it will not be taken away from her."

Jesus Teaches about Prayer

11 One day Jesus was praying in a certain place. When he finished, one of his disciples spoke to him. "Lord," he said, "teach us to pray, just as John taught his disciples."

² Jesus said to them, "When you pray, this is what you should say.

" 'Father,
may your name be honoured.
May your kingdom come.
³ Give us each day our daily bread.
⁴ Forgive us our sins,
    as we also forgive everyone who sins against us.
Keep us from falling into sin when we are tempted.' "

⁵ Then Jesus said to them, "Suppose you have a friend. You go to him at midnight and say, 'Friend, lend me three loaves of bread. ⁶ A friend of mine on a journey has come to stay with me. I have no food to give him.' ⁷ And suppose the one inside answers, 'Don't bother me. The door is already locked. My children and I are in bed. I can't get up and give you anything.' ⁸ I tell you, that person will not get up. And he won't give you bread just because he is your friend. But because you keep bothering him, he will surely get up. He will give you as much as you need.

⁹ "So here is what I say to you. Ask, and it will be given to you. Search, and you will find. Knock, and the door will be opened to you. ¹⁰ Everyone who asks will receive. The one who searches will find. And the door will be opened to the one who knocks.

¹¹ "Fathers, suppose your son asks for a fish. Which of you will give him a snake instead? ¹² Or suppose he asks for an egg. Which of you will give him a scorpion? ¹³ Even though you are evil, you know how to give good gifts to your children. How much more will your Father who is in heaven give the Holy Spirit to those who ask him!"

Jesus and Beelzebul

[14] Jesus was driving out a demon. The man who had the demon could not speak. When the demon left, the man began to speak. The crowd was amazed. [15] But some of them said, "Jesus is driving out demons by the power of Beelzebul, the prince of demons." [16] Others tested Jesus by asking for a sign from heaven.

[17] Jesus knew what they were thinking. So he said to them, "Any kingdom that fights against itself will be destroyed. A family that is divided against itself will fall. [18] If Satan fights against himself, how can his kingdom stand? I say this because of what you claim. You say I drive out demons by the power of Beelzebul. [19] Suppose I do drive out demons with Beelzebul's help. With whose help do your followers drive them out? So then, they will be your judges. [20] But suppose I drive out demons with the help of God's powerful finger. Then God's kingdom has come upon you.

[21] "When a strong man is completely armed and guards his house, what he owns is safe. [22] But when someone stronger attacks, he is overpowered. The attacker takes away the armour the man had trusted in. Then he divides up what he has stolen.

[23] "Whoever is not with me is against me. And whoever does not gather with me scatters.

[24] "What happens when an evil spirit comes out of a person? It goes through dry areas looking for a place to rest. But it doesn't find it. Then it says, 'I will return to the house I left.' [25] When it arrives there, it finds the house swept clean and put in order. [26] Then the evil spirit goes and takes seven other spirits more evil than itself. They go in and live there. That person is worse off than before."

[27] As Jesus was saying these things, a woman in the crowd called out. She shouted, "Blessed is the mother who gave you birth and fed you."

[28] He replied, "Instead, blessed are those who hear God's word and obey it."

The Sign of Jonah

[29] As the crowds grew larger, Jesus spoke to them. "The people of today are evil," he said. "They ask for a sign from God. But

none will be given except the sign of Jonah. [30] He was a sign from God to the people of Nineveh. In the same way, the Son of Man will be a sign from God to the people of today. [31] The Queen of the South will stand up on judgment day with the people now living. And she will prove that they are guilty. She came from very far away to listen to Solomon's wisdom. And now something more important than Solomon is here. [32] The men of Nineveh will stand up on judgment day with the people now living. And the Ninevites will prove that those people are guilty. The men of Nineveh turned away from their sins when Jonah preached to them. And now something more important than Jonah is here.

The Eye Is the Lamp of the Body

[33] "No-one lights a lamp and hides it. No-one puts it under a bowl. Instead, they put a lamp on its stand. Then those who come in can see the light. [34] Your eye is like a lamp for your body. Suppose your eyes are healthy. Then your whole body also is full of light. But suppose your eyes can't see well. Then your body also is full of darkness. [35] So make sure that the light inside you is not darkness. [36] Suppose your whole body is full of light. And suppose no part of it is dark. Then your body will be full of light. It will be just as when a lamp shines its light on you."

Six Warnings

[37] Jesus finished speaking. Then a Pharisee invited him to eat with him. So Jesus went in and took his place at the table. [38] But the Pharisee was surprised. He noticed that Jesus did not wash before the meal.

[39] Then the Lord spoke to him. "You Pharisees clean the outside of the cup and dish," he said. "But inside you are full of greed and evil. [40] You foolish people! Didn't the one who made the outside make the inside also? [41] Give freely to poor people to show what is inside you. Then everything will be clean for you.

[42] "How terrible it will be for you Pharisees! You give God a tenth of your garden plants, such as mint and rue. But you have forgotten to be fair and to love God. You should have practised the last things without failing to do the first.

⁴³ "How terrible for you Pharisees! You love the most important seats in the synagogues. You love having people greet you with respect in the market.

⁴⁴ "How terrible for you! You are like graves that are not marked. People walk over them without knowing it."

⁴⁵ An authority on the law spoke to Jesus. He said, "Teacher, when you say things like that, you say bad things about us too."

⁴⁶ Jesus replied, "How terrible for you authorities on the law! You put such heavy loads on people that they can hardly carry them. But you yourselves will not lift one finger to help them.

⁴⁷ "How terrible for you! You build tombs for the prophets. It was your people of long ago who killed them. ⁴⁸ So you show that you agree with what your people did long ago. They killed the prophets, and now you build the prophets' tombs. ⁴⁹ So God in his wisdom said, 'I will send prophets and apostles to them. They will kill some. And they will try to hurt others.' ⁵⁰ So the people of today will be punished. They will pay for all the prophets' blood spilled since the world began. ⁵¹ I mean from the blood of Abel to the blood of Zechariah. He was killed between the altar and the temple. Yes, I tell you, the people of today will be punished for all these things.

⁵² "How terrible for you authorities on the law! You have taken away the key to the door of knowledge. You yourselves have not entered. And you have stood in the way of those who were entering."

⁵³ When Jesus went outside, the Pharisees and the teachers of the law strongly opposed him. They threw a lot of questions at him. ⁵⁴ They set traps for him. They wanted to catch him in something he might say.

Jesus Gives Words of Warning and Hope

12 During that time a crowd of many thousands had gathered. There were so many people that they were stepping on one another. Jesus spoke first to his disciples. "Be on your guard against the yeast of the Pharisees," he said. "They just pretend to be godly. ² Everything that is secret will be brought out into the open. Everything that is hidden will be uncovered. ³ What you have said in the dark will be heard in the

daylight. What you have whispered to someone behind closed doors will be shouted from the rooftops.

⁴ "My friends, listen to me. Don't be afraid of those who kill the body but can't do any more than that. ⁵ I will show you whom you should be afraid of. Be afraid of the one who has the authority to throw you into hell after you have been killed. Yes, I tell you, be afraid of him. ⁶ Aren't five sparrows sold for two pennies? But God does not forget even one of them. ⁷ In fact, he even counts every hair on your head! So don't be afraid. You are worth more than many sparrows.

⁸ "What about someone who says in front of others that he knows me? I tell you, the Son of Man will say in front of God's angels that he knows that person. ⁹ But what about someone who says in front of others that he doesn't know me? I, the Son of Man, will say in front of God's angels that I don't know him. ¹⁰ Everyone who speaks a word against the Son of Man will be forgiven. But anyone who speaks evil things against the Holy Spirit will not be forgiven.

¹¹ "You will be brought before synagogues, rulers and authorities. But do not worry about how to stand up for yourselves or what to say. ¹² The Holy Spirit will teach you at that time what you should say."

The Story of the Rich Fool

¹³ Someone in the crowd spoke to Jesus. "Teacher," he said, "tell my brother to divide the family property with me."

¹⁴ Jesus replied, "Friend, who made me a judge or umpire between you?" ¹⁵ Then he said to them, "Watch out! Be on your guard against wanting to have more and more things. Life is not made up of how much a person has."

¹⁶ Then Jesus told them a story. He said, "A certain rich man's land produced a very large crop. ¹⁷ He thought to himself, 'What should I do? I don't have any place to store my crops.'

¹⁸ "Then he said, 'This is what I'll do. I will tear down my barns and build bigger ones. I will store my extra corn in them. ¹⁹ I'll say to myself, "You have plenty of corn stored away for many years. Take life easy. Eat, drink and have a good time." '

20 "But God said to him, 'You foolish man! Tonight I will take your life away from you. Then who will get what you have prepared for yourself?'

21 "That is how it will be for whoever stores things away for themselves but is not rich in the sight of God."

Do Not Worry

22 Then Jesus spoke to his disciples. He said, "I tell you, do not worry. Don't worry about your life and what you will eat. And don't worry about your body and what you will wear. 23 There is more to life than eating. There are more important things for the body than clothes. 24 Think about the ravens. They don't plant or gather crops. They don't have any barns at all. But God feeds them. You are worth much more than birds! 25 Can you add even one hour to your life by worrying? 26 You can't do that very little thing. So why worry about the rest?

27 "Think about how the wild flowers grow. They don't work or make clothing. But here is what I tell you. Not even Solomon in his royal robes was dressed like one of those flowers. 28 If that is how God dresses the wild grass, how much better will he dress you! After all, the grass is here only today. Tomorrow it is thrown into the fire. Your faith is so small! 29 Don't spend time thinking about what you will eat or drink. Don't worry about it. 30 People who are ungodly run after all those things. Your Father knows that you need them. 31 But put God's kingdom first. Then those other things will also be given to you.

32 "Little flock, do not be afraid. Your Father has been pleased to give you the kingdom. 33 Sell what you own. Give to those who are poor. Provide purses for yourselves that will not wear out. Store up riches in heaven that will never be used up. There, no thief can come near it. There, no moth can destroy it. 34 Your heart will be where your riches are.

Be Ready

35 "Be dressed and ready to serve. Keep your lamps burning. 36 Be like servants waiting for their master to return from a wedding dinner. When he comes and knocks, they can open the

door for him at once. [37] It will be good for those servants whose master finds them ready when he comes. What I'm about to tell you is true. The master will then dress himself so he can serve them. He will have them take their places at the table. And he will come and wait on them. [38] It will be good for those servants whose master finds them ready. It will even be good if he comes in the middle of the night or towards morning. [39] But here is what you must understand. Suppose the owner of the house knew at what hour the robber was coming. He would not have let his house be broken into. [40] You also must be ready. The Son of Man will come at an hour when you don't expect him."

[41] Peter asked, "Lord, are you telling this story to us, or to everyone?"

[42] The Lord answered, "Suppose a master puts one of his servants in charge of his other servants. The servant's job is to give them the food they are to receive at the right time. The master wants a faithful and wise manager for this. [43] It will be good for the servant if the master finds him doing his job when the master returns. [44] What I'm about to tell you is true. The master will put that servant in charge of everything he owns. [45] But suppose the servant says to himself, 'My master is taking a long time to come back.' Suppose that servant begins to beat the other servants, both men and women. Suppose he feeds himself. And suppose he drinks until he gets drunk. [46] The master of that servant will come back on a day the servant doesn't expect him. The master will return at an hour the servant doesn't know. Then the master will cut him to pieces. He will send the servant to the place where unbelievers go.

[47] "Suppose a servant knows the master's wishes. But the servant doesn't get ready and doesn't do what the master wants. Then that servant will receive a heavy beating. [48] But suppose the servant does not know his master's wishes. And suppose the servant does things for which he should be punished. He will receive a lighter beating. "Much will be required of everyone who has been given much. Even more will be asked of the person who is supposed to take care of much.

Jesus Will Separate People from One Another

⁴⁹ "I have come to bring fire on the earth. How I wish the fire had already started! ⁵⁰ But I have a baptism of suffering to go through. And I must go through it. ⁵¹ Do you think I came to bring peace on earth? No, I tell you. I have come to separate people. ⁵² From now on there will be five members in a family, each one against the other. There will be three against two and two against three. ⁵³ They will be separated. Father will turn against son and son against father. Mother will turn against daughter and daughter against mother. Mother in law will turn against daughter-in-law and daughter-in-law against mother in law."

Understanding the Meaning of What Is Happening

⁵⁴ Jesus spoke to the crowd. He said, "You see a cloud rising in the west. Right away you say, 'It's going to rain.' And it does. ⁵⁵ The south wind blows. So you say, 'It's going to be hot.' And it is. ⁵⁶ You pretenders! You know how to understand the appearance of the earth and the sky. Why can't you understand the meaning of what is happening right now?

⁵⁷ "Why don't you judge for yourselves what is right? ⁵⁸ Suppose someone has a claim against you, and you are on your way to court. Try hard to settle the matter on the way. If you don't, that person may drag you off to the judge. The judge may turn you over to the officer. And the officer may throw you into prison. ⁵⁹ I tell you, you will not get out until you have paid the very last penny!"

Turn Away from Sin or Die

13 Some people who were there at that time told Jesus about certain Galileans. Pilate had mixed their blood with their sacrifices. ² Jesus said, "These people from Galilee suffered greatly. Do you think they were worse sinners than all the other Galileans? ³ I tell you, no! But unless you turn away from your sins, you will all die too. ⁴ Or what about the 18 people in Siloam? They died when the tower fell on them. Do you think they were more guilty than all the others living in Jerusalem?

⁵ I tell you, no! But unless you turn away from your sins, you will all die too."

⁶ Then Jesus told a story. "A man had a fig tree," he said. "It was growing in his vineyard. When he went to look for fruit on it, he didn't find any. ⁷ So he went to the man who took care of the vineyard. He said, 'For three years now I've been coming to look for fruit on this fig tree. But I haven't found any. Cut it down! Why should it use up the soil?'

⁸ " 'Sir,' the man replied, 'leave it alone for one more year. I'll dig around it and feed it. ⁹ If it bears fruit next year, fine! If not, then cut it down.' "

Jesus Heals a Disabled Woman on the Sabbath Day

¹⁰ Jesus was teaching in one of the synagogues on a Sabbath day. ¹¹ A woman there had been disabled by an evil spirit for 18 years. She was bent over and could not stand up straight. ¹² Jesus saw her. He asked her to come to him. He said to her, "Woman, you will no longer be disabled. I am about to set you free." ¹³ Then he put his hands on her. Right away she stood up straight and praised God.

¹⁴ Jesus had healed the woman on the Sabbath day. This made the synagogue leader angry. He told the people, "There are six days for work. So come and be healed on those days. But do not come on the Sabbath day."

¹⁵ The Lord answered him, "You pretenders! Doesn't each of you go to the barn and untie your ox or donkey on the Sabbath day? Then don't you lead it out to give it water? ¹⁶ This woman is a member of Abraham's family line. But Satan has kept her disabled for 18 long years. Shouldn't she be set free on the Sabbath day from what was keeping her disabled?"

¹⁷ When Jesus said this, all those who opposed him were put to shame. But the people were delighted. They loved all the wonderful things he was doing.

The Stories of the Mustard Seed and the Yeast

¹⁸ Then Jesus asked, "What is God's kingdom like? What can I compare it to? ¹⁹ It is like a mustard seed. Someone took the

seed and planted it in a garden. It grew and became a tree. The birds sat in its branches."

²⁰ Again he asked, "What can I compare God's kingdom to? ²¹ It is like yeast that a woman used. She mixed it into 60 pounds of flour. The yeast worked its way all through the dough."

The Narrow Door

²² Then Jesus went through the towns and villages, teaching the people. He was on his way to Jerusalem. ²³ Someone asked him, "Lord, are only a few people going to be saved?"

He said to them, ²⁴ "Try very hard to enter through the narrow door. I tell you, many will try to enter and will not be able to. ²⁵ The owner of the house will get up and close the door. Then you will stand outside knocking and begging. You will say, 'Sir, open the door for us.'

"But he will answer, 'I don't know you. And I don't know where you come from.'

²⁶ "Then you will say, 'We ate and drank with you. You taught in our streets.'

²⁷ "But he will reply, 'I don't know you. And I don't know where you come from. Get away from me, all you who do evil!'

²⁸ "You will weep and grind your teeth together when you see those who are in God's kingdom. You will see Abraham, Isaac and Jacob and all the prophets there. But you yourselves will be thrown out. ²⁹ People will come from east and west and north and south. They will take their places at the feast in God's kingdom. ³⁰ Then the last will be first. And the first will be last."

Jesus' Sadness over Jerusalem

³¹ At that time some Pharisees came to Jesus. They said to him, "Leave this place. Go somewhere else. Herod wants to kill you."

³² He replied, "Go and tell that fox, 'I will keep on driving out demons. I will keep on healing people today and tomorrow. And on the third day I will reach my goal.' ³³ In any case, I must keep going today and tomorrow and the next day. Certainly no prophet can die outside Jerusalem!

³⁴ "Jerusalem! Jerusalem! You kill the prophets and throw

stones in order to kill those who are sent to you. Many times I have wanted to gather your people together. I have wanted to be like a hen who gathers her chicks under her wings. And you would not let me. ³⁵ Look, your house is left empty. I tell you, you will not see me again until you say, 'Blessed is the one who comes in the name of the Lord.' " *(Psalm 118:26)*

Jesus Eats at a Pharisee's House

14 One Sabbath day, Jesus went to eat in the house of a well known Pharisee. While he was there, he was being carefully watched. ² In front of him was a man whose body was badly swollen. ³ Jesus turned to the Pharisees and the authorities on the law. He asked them, "Is it breaking the Law to heal on the Sabbath day?" ⁴ But they remained silent. So Jesus took hold of the man and healed him. Then he sent him away.

⁵ He asked them another question. He said, "Suppose one of you has a child or an ox that falls into a well on the Sabbath day. Wouldn't you pull it out right away?" ⁶ And they had nothing to say.

⁷ Jesus noticed how the guests picked the places of honour at the table. So he told them a story. ⁸ He said, "Suppose someone invites you to a wedding feast. Do not take the place of honour. A person more important than you may have been invited. ⁹ If so, the host who invited both of you will come to you. He will say, 'Give this person your seat.' Then you will be filled with shame. You will have to take the least important place. ¹⁰ But when you are invited, take the lowest place. Then your host will come over to you. He will say, 'Friend, move up to a better place.' Then you will be honoured in front of all the other guests. ¹¹ All those who lift themselves up will be made humble. And those who make themselves humble will be lifted up."

¹² Then Jesus spoke to his host. "Suppose you give a lunch or a dinner," he said. "Do not invite your friends, your brothers or sisters, or your relatives, or your rich neighbours. If you do, they may invite you to eat with them. So you will be paid back. ¹³ But when you give a banquet, invite those who are poor. Also invite those who can't see or walk. ¹⁴ Then you will be blessed. Your guests can't pay you back. But you will be paid back when those who are right with God rise from the dead."

The Story of the Great Banquet

¹⁵ One of the people at the table with Jesus heard him say those things. So he said to Jesus, "Blessed is the one who will eat at the feast in God's kingdom."

¹⁶ Jesus replied, "A certain man was preparing a great banquet. He invited many guests. ¹⁷ Then the day of the banquet arrived. He sent his servant to those who had been invited. The servant told them, 'Come. Everything is ready now.'

¹⁸ "But they all had the same idea. They began to make excuses. The first one said, 'I have just bought a field. I have to go and see it. Please excuse me.'

¹⁹ "Another said, 'I have just bought five pairs of oxen. I'm on my way to try them out. Please excuse me.'

²⁰ "Still another said, 'I just got married, so I can't come.'

²¹ "The servant came back and reported this to his master. "Then the owner of the house became angry. He ordered his servant, 'Go out quickly into the streets and lanes of the town. Bring in those who are poor. Also bring those who can't see or walk.'

²² " 'Sir,' the servant said, 'what you ordered has been done. But there is still room.'

²³ "Then the master told his servant, 'Go out to the roads. Go out to the country lanes. Make the people come in. I want my house to be full. ²⁴ I tell you, not one of those people who were invited will get a taste of my banquet.' "

The Cost of Being a Disciple

²⁵ Large crowds were travelling with Jesus. He turned and spoke to them. He said, ²⁶ "Anyone who comes to me must hate their father and mother. They must hate their wife and children. They must hate their brothers and sisters. And they must hate even their own life. Unless they do this, they can't be my disciple. ²⁷ Whoever doesn't carry their cross and follow me can't be my disciple.

²⁸ "Suppose one of you wants to build a tower. Won't you sit down first and figure out how much it will cost? Then you will see whether you have enough money to finish it. ²⁹ Suppose you

start building and are not able to finish. Then everyone who sees what you have done will laugh at you. [30] They will say, 'This person started to build but wasn't able to finish.'

[31] "Or suppose a king is about to go to war against another king. And suppose he has 10,000 men, while the other has 20,000 coming against him. Won't he first sit down and think about whether he can win? [32] And suppose he decides he can't win. Then he will send some men to ask how peace can be made. He will do this while the other king is still far away. [33] In the same way, you must give up everything you have. Those of you who don't cannot be my disciple.

[34] "Salt is good. But suppose it loses its saltiness. How can it be made salty again? [35] It is not good for the soil. And it is not good for the trash pile. It will be thrown out.

"Whoever has ears should listen."

The Story of the Lost Sheep

15 The tax collectors and sinners were all gathering around to hear Jesus. [2] But the Pharisees and the teachers of the law were whispering among themselves. They said, "This man welcomes sinners and eats with them."

[3] Then Jesus told them a story. [4] He said, "Suppose one of you has 100 sheep and loses one of them. Won't he leave the 99 in the open country? Won't he go and look for the one lost sheep until he finds it? [5] When he finds it, he will joyfully put it on his shoulders [6] and go home. Then he will call his friends and neighbours together. He will say, 'Be joyful with me. I have found my lost sheep.' [7] I tell you, it will be the same in heaven. There will be great joy when one sinner turns away from sin. Yes, there will be more joy than for 99 godly people who do not need to turn away from their sins.

The Story of the Lost Coin

[8] "Or suppose a woman has ten silver coins and loses one. Won't she light a lamp and sweep the house? Won't she search carefully until she finds the coin? [9] And when she finds it, she will call her friends and neighbours together. She will say, 'Be joyful with me. I have found my lost coin.' [10] I tell you, it is the same in

heaven. There is joy in heaven over one sinner who turns away from sin."

The Story of the Lost Son

¹¹ Jesus continued, "There was a man who had two sons.
¹² The younger son spoke to his father. He said, 'Father, give me my share of the family property.' So the father divided his property between his two sons.

¹³ "Not long after that, the younger son packed up all he had. Then he left for a country far away. There he wasted his money on wild living. ¹⁴ He spent everything he had. "Then the whole country ran low on food. So the son didn't have what he needed. ¹⁵ He went to work for someone who lived in that country. That person sent the son to the fields to feed the pigs. ¹⁶ The son wanted to fill his stomach with the food the pigs were eating. But no-one gave him anything.

¹⁷ "Then he began to think clearly again. He said, 'How many of my father's hired servants have more than enough food! But here I am dying from hunger! ¹⁸ I will get up and go back to my father. I will say to him, "Father, I have sinned against heaven. And I have sinned against you. ¹⁹ I am no longer fit to be called your son. Make me like one of your hired servants." ' ²⁰ So he got up and went to his father.

"While the son was still a long way off, his father saw him. He was filled with tender love for his son. He ran to him. He threw his arms around him and kissed him.

²¹ "The son said to him, 'Father, I have sinned against heaven and against you. I am no longer fit to be called your son.'

²² "But the father said to his servants, 'Quick! Bring the best robe and put it on him. Put a ring on his finger and sandals on his feet. ²³ Bring the fattest calf and kill it. Let's have a feast and celebrate. ²⁴ This son of mine was dead. And now he is alive again. He was lost. And now he is found.' "So they began to celebrate.

²⁵ "The elder son was in the field. When he came near the house, he heard music and dancing. ²⁶ So he called one of the servants. He asked him what was going on. ²⁷ 'Your brother has come home,' the servant replied. 'Your father has killed the

fattest calf. He has done this because your brother is back safe and sound.'

²⁸ "The older brother became angry. He refused to go in. So his father went out and begged him. ²⁹ But he answered his father, 'Look! All these years I've worked like a slave for you. I have always obeyed your orders. You never gave me even a young goat so I could celebrate with my friends. ³⁰ But this son of yours wasted your money with some prostitutes. Now he comes home. And for him you kill the fattest calf!'

³¹ " 'My son,' the father said, 'you are always with me. Everything I have is yours. ³² But we had to celebrate and be glad. This brother of yours was dead. And now he is alive again. He was lost. And now he is found.' "

The Story of the Clever Manager

16 Jesus told his disciples another story. He said, "There was a rich man who had a manager. Some said that the manager was wasting what the rich man owned. ² So the rich man told him to come in. He asked him, 'What is this I hear about you? Tell me exactly how you have handled what I own. You can't be my manager any longer.'

³ "The manager said to himself, 'What will I do now? My master is taking away my job. I'm not strong enough to dig. And I'm too ashamed to beg. ⁴ I know what I'm going to do. I'll do something so that when I lose my job here, people will welcome me into their houses.'

⁵ "So he called in each person who owed his master something. He asked the first one, 'How much do you owe my master?'

⁶ " 'I owe 900 gallons of olive oil,' he replied.

"The manager told him, 'Take your bill. Sit down quickly and change it to 450 gallons.'

⁷ "Then he asked the second one, 'And how much do you owe?'

" 'I owe 1,000 bushels of wheat,' he replied.

"The manager told him, 'Take your bill and change it to 800 bushels.'

⁸ "The manager had not been honest. But the master praised him for being clever. The people of this world are clever in dealing with those who are like themselves. They are more

clever than God's people. [9] I tell you, use the riches of this world to help others. In that way, you will make friends for yourselves. Then when your riches are gone, you will be welcomed into your eternal home in heaven.

[10] "Suppose you can be trusted with very little. Then you can be trusted with a lot. But suppose you are not honest with very little. Then you will not be honest with a lot. [11] Suppose you have not been worthy of trust in handling worldly wealth. Then who will trust you with true riches? [12] Suppose you have not been worthy of trust in handling someone else's property. Then who will give you property of your own?

[13] "No-one can serve two masters at the same time. Either you will hate one of them and love the other. Or you will be faithful to one and dislike the other. You can't serve God and money at the same time."

[14] The Pharisees loved money. They heard all that Jesus said and made fun of him. [15] Jesus said to them, "You try to make yourselves look good in the eyes of other people. But God knows your hearts. What people think is worth a lot is hated by God.

More Teachings

[16] "The teachings of the Law and the Prophets were preached until John the Baptist came. Since then, the good news of God's kingdom is being preached. And everyone is trying very hard to enter it. [17] It is easier for heaven and earth to disappear than for the smallest part of a letter to drop out of the Law.

[18] "Anyone who divorces his wife and marries another woman commits adultery. Also, the man who marries a divorced woman commits adultery.

The Rich Man and Lazarus

[19] "Once there was a rich man. He was dressed in purple cloth and fine linen. He lived an easy life every day. [20] A man named Lazarus was placed at his gate. Lazarus was a beggar. His body was covered with sores. [21] Even dogs came and licked his sores. All he wanted was to eat what fell from the rich man's table.

[22] "The time came when the beggar died. The angels carried him to Abraham's side. The rich man also died and was buried.

²³ In the place of the dead, the rich man was suffering terribly. He looked up and saw Abraham far away. Lazarus was by his side. ²⁴ So the rich man called out, 'Father Abraham! Have pity on me! Send Lazarus to dip the tip of his finger in water. Then he can cool my tongue with it. I am in terrible pain in this fire.'

²⁵ "But Abraham replied, 'Son, remember what happened in your lifetime. You received your good things. Lazarus received bad things. Now he is comforted here, and you are in terrible pain. ²⁶ Besides, a wide space has been placed between us and you. So those who want to go from here to you can't go. And no-one can cross over from there to us.'

²⁷ "The rich man answered, 'Then I beg you, father Abraham. Send Lazarus to my family. ²⁸ I have five brothers. Let Lazarus warn them. Then they will not come to this place of terrible suffering.'

²⁹ "Abraham replied, 'They have the teachings of Moses and the Prophets. Let your brothers listen to them.'

³⁰ " 'No, father Abraham,' he said. 'But if someone from the dead goes to them, they will turn away from their sins.'

³¹ "Abraham said to him, 'They do not listen to Moses and the Prophets. So they will not be convinced even if someone rises from the dead.' "

Sin, Faith and Duty

17 Jesus spoke to his disciples. "Things that make people sin are sure to come," he said. "But how terrible it will be for anyone who causes those things to come! ² Suppose people lead one of these little ones to sin. It would be better for those people to be thrown into the sea with a millstone tied around their neck. ³ So watch what you do.

"If your brother or sister sins against you, tell them they are wrong. Then if they turn away from their sins, forgive them. ⁴ Suppose they sin against you seven times in one day. And suppose they come back to you each time and say, 'I'm sorry.' You must forgive them."

⁵ The apostles said to the Lord, "Give us more faith!"

⁶ He replied, "Suppose you have faith as small as a mustard seed. Then you can say to this mulberry tree, 'Be pulled up. Be planted in the sea.' And it will obey you.

[7] "Suppose one of you has a servant ploughing or looking after the sheep. And suppose the servant came in from the field. Will you say to him, 'Come along now and sit down to eat'? [8] No. Instead, you will say, 'Prepare my supper. Get yourself ready. Wait on me while I eat and drink. Then after that you can eat and drink.' [9] Will you thank the servant because he did what he was told to do? [10] It's the same with you. Suppose you have done everything you were told to do. Then you should say, 'We are not worthy to serve you. We have only done our duty.'"

Jesus Heals Ten Men Who Have a Skin Disease

[11] Jesus was on his way to Jerusalem. He travelled along the border between Samaria and Galilee. [12] As he was going into a village, ten men met him. They had a skin disease. They were standing close by. [13] And they called out in a loud voice, "Jesus! Master! Have pity on us!"

[14] Jesus saw them and said, "Go. Show yourselves to the priests." While they were on the way, they were healed.

[15] When one of them saw that he was healed, he came back. He praised God in a loud voice. [16] He threw himself at Jesus' feet and thanked him. The man was a Samaritan.

[17] Jesus asked, "Weren't all ten healed? Where are the other nine? [18] Didn't anyone else return and give praise to God except this outsider?" [19] Then Jesus said to him, "Get up and go. Your faith has healed you."

The Coming of God's Kingdom

[20] Once the Pharisees asked Jesus when God's kingdom would come. He replied, "The coming of God's kingdom is not something you can see. [21] People will not say, 'Here it is.' Or, 'There it is.' That's because God's kingdom is among you."

[22] Then Jesus spoke to his disciples. "The time is coming," he said, "when you will long to see one of the days of the Son of Man. But you won't see it. [23] People will tell you, 'There he is!' Or, 'Here he is!' Don't go running off after them. [24] When the Son of Man comes, he will be like the lightning. It flashes and lights up the sky from one end to the other. [25] But first the Son of Man

must suffer many things. He will not be accepted by the people of today.

26 "Remember how it was in the days of Noah. It will be the same when the Son of Man comes. 27 People were eating and drinking. They were getting married. They were giving their daughters to be married. They did all those things right up to the day Noah entered the ark. Then the flood came and destroyed them all.

28 "It was the same in the days of Lot. People were eating and drinking. They were buying and selling. They were planting and building. 29 But on the day Lot left Sodom, fire and sulphur rained down from heaven. And all the people were destroyed.

30 "It will be just like that on the day the Son of Man is shown to the world. 31 Suppose someone is on the housetop on that day. And suppose what they own is inside the house. They should not go down to get what they own. No-one in the field should go back for anything either. 32 Remember Lot's wife! 33 Whoever tries to keep their life will lose it. Whoever loses their life will keep it. 34 I tell you, on that night two people will be in one bed. One person will be taken and the other left. 35-36 Two women will be grinding corn together. One will be taken and the other left."

37 "Where, Lord?" his disciples asked.

He replied, "The vultures will gather where there is a dead body."

The Story of the Widow Who Would Not Give Up

18 Jesus told his disciples a story. He wanted to show them that they should always pray and not give up. 2 He said, "In a certain town there was a judge. He didn't have any respect for God or care about what people thought. 3 A widow lived in that town. She came to the judge again and again. She kept begging him, 'Make things right for me. Someone is treating me badly.'

4 "For some time the judge refused. But finally he said to himself, 'I don't have any respect for God. I don't care about what people think. 5 But this widow keeps bothering me. So I will see that things are made right for her. If I don't, she will someday come and attack me!'"

6 The Lord said, "Listen to what the unfair judge says. 7 God's chosen people cry out to him day and night. Won't he make

things right for them? Will he keep putting them off? [8] I tell you, God will see that things are made right for them. He will make sure it happens quickly. "But when the Son of Man comes, will he find people on earth who have faith?"

The Story of the Pharisee and the Tax Collector

[9] Jesus told a story to some people who were sure they were right with God. They looked down on everyone else. [10] He said to them, "Two men went up to the temple to pray. One was a Pharisee. The other was a tax collector. [11] The Pharisee stood by himself and prayed. 'God, I thank you that I am not like other people,' he said. 'I am not like robbers or those who do other evil things. I am not like those who commit adultery. I am not even like this tax collector. [12] I fast twice a week. And I give a tenth of all I get.'

[13] "But the tax collector stood not very far away. He would not even look up to heaven. He brought his hand to his heart and prayed. He said, 'God, have mercy on me. I am a sinner.'

[14] "I tell you, the tax collector went home accepted by God. But not the Pharisee. All those who lift themselves up will be made humble. And those who make themselves humble will be lifted up."

Little Children Are Brought to Jesus

[15] People were also bringing babies to Jesus. They wanted him to place his hands on the babies. When the disciples saw this, they told the people to stop. [16] But Jesus asked the children to come to him. "Let the little children come to me," he said. "Don't keep them away. God's kingdom belongs to people like them. [17] What I'm about to tell you is true. Anyone who will not receive God's kingdom like a little child will never enter it."

Rich People and the Kingdom of God

[18] A certain ruler asked Jesus a question. "Good teacher," he said, "what must I do to receive eternal life?"

[19] "Why do you call me good?" Jesus answered. "No-one is good except God. [20] You know what the commandments say.

'Do not commit adultery. Do not commit murder. Do not steal. Do not be a false witness. Honour your father and mother.' "
(Exodus 20:12-16; Deuteronomy 5:16-20)

²¹ "I have obeyed all those commandments since I was a boy," the ruler said.

²² When Jesus heard this, he said to him, "You are still missing one thing. Sell everything you have. Give the money to those who are poor. You will have treasure in heaven. Then come and follow me."

²³ When the ruler heard this, he became very sad. He was very rich. ²⁴ Jesus looked at him. Then he said, "How hard it is for rich people to enter God's kingdom! ²⁵ Is it hard for a camel to go through the eye of a needle? It is even harder for someone who is rich to enter God's kingdom!"

²⁶ Those who heard this asked, "Then who can be saved?"

²⁷ Jesus replied, "Things that are impossible with people are possible with God."

²⁸ Peter said to him, "We have left everything we had in order to follow you!"

²⁹ "What I'm about to tell you is true," Jesus said to them. "Has anyone left home or wife or husband or brothers or sisters or parents or children for God's kingdom? ³⁰ They will receive many times as much in this world. In the world to come they will receive eternal life."

Jesus Speaks a Third Time about His Coming Death

³¹ Jesus took the 12 disciples to one side. He told them, "We are going up to Jerusalem. Everything that the prophets wrote about the Son of Man will come true. ³² He will be handed over to the Gentiles. They will make fun of him. They will laugh at him and spit on him. ³³ They will whip him and kill him. On the third day, he will rise from the dead!"

³⁴ The disciples did not understand any of this. Its meaning was hidden from them. So they didn't know what Jesus was talking about.

A Blind Beggar Receives His Sight

³⁵ Jesus was approaching Jericho. A blind man was sitting by

the side of the road begging. [36] The blind man heard the crowd going by. He asked what was happening. [37] They told him, "Jesus of Nazareth is passing by."

[38] So the blind man called out, "Jesus! Son of David! Have mercy on me!"

[39] Those who led the way commanded him to stop. They told him to be quiet. But he shouted even louder, "Son of David! Have mercy on me!"

[40] Jesus stopped and ordered the man to be brought to him. When the man came near, Jesus spoke to him. [41] "What do you want me to do for you?" Jesus asked.

"Lord, I want to be able to see," the blind man replied.

[42] Jesus said to him, "Receive your sight. Your faith has healed you." [43] Right away he could see. He followed Jesus, praising God. When all the people saw it, they also praised God.

Zacchaeus the Tax Collector

19 Jesus entered Jericho and was passing through. [2] A man named Zacchaeus lived there. He was a chief tax collector and was very rich. [3] Zacchaeus wanted to see who Jesus was. But he was a short man. He could not see Jesus because of the crowd. [4] So he ran ahead and climbed a sycamore fig tree. He wanted to see Jesus, who was coming that way.

[5] Jesus reached the spot where Zacchaeus was. He looked up and said, "Zacchaeus, come down at once. I must stay at your house today." [6] So Zacchaeus came down at once and welcomed him gladly.

[7] All the people saw this. They began to whisper among themselves. They said, "Jesus has gone to be the guest of a sinner."

[8] But Zacchaeus stood up. He said, "Look, Lord! Here and now I give half of what I own to those who are poor. And if I have cheated anybody out of anything, I will pay it back. I will pay back four times the amount I took."

[9] Jesus said to Zacchaeus, "Today salvation has come to your house. You are a member of Abraham's family line. [10] The Son of Man came to look for the lost and save them."

The Story of Three Slaves

[11] While the people were listening to these things, Jesus told them a story. He was near Jerusalem. The people thought that God's kingdom was going to appear right away. [12] Jesus said, "A man from an important family went to a country far away. He went there to be made king and then return home. [13] So he sent for ten of his slaves. He gave them each about three months' pay. 'Put this money to work until I come back,' he said.

[14] "But those he ruled over hated him. They sent some messengers after him. They were sent to say, 'We don't want this man to be our king.'

[15] "But he was made king and returned home. Then he sent for the slaves he had given the money to. He wanted to find out what they had earned with it.

[16] "The first one came to him. He said, 'Sir, your money has earned ten times as much.'

[17] " 'You have done well, my good slave!' his master replied. 'You have been faithful in a very small matter. So I will put you in charge of ten towns.'

[18] "The second slave came to his master. He said, 'Sir, your money has earned five times as much.'

[19] "His master answered, 'I will put you in charge of five towns.'

[20] "Then another slave came. He said, 'Sir, here is your money. I have kept it hidden in a piece of cloth. [21] I was afraid of you. You are a hard man. You take out what you did not put in. You harvest what you did not plant.'

[22] "His master replied, 'I will judge you by your own words, you evil slave! So you knew that I am a hard man? You knew that I take out what I did not put in? You knew that I harvest what I did not plant? [23] Then why didn't you put my money in the bank? When I came back, I could have collected it with interest.'

[24] "Then he said to those standing by, 'Take his money away from him. Give it to the one who has ten times as much.'

[25] " 'Sir,' they said, 'he already has ten times as much!'

[26] "He replied, 'I tell you that everyone who has will be given more. But here is what will happen to anyone who has nothing. Even what they have will be taken away from them. [27] And what

about my enemies who did not want me to be king over them? Bring them here! Kill them in front of me!' "

Jesus Comes to Jerusalem as King

²⁸ After Jesus had said this, he went on ahead. He was going up to Jerusalem. ²⁹ He approached Bethphage and Bethany. The hill there was called the Mount of Olives. Jesus sent out two of his disciples. He said to them, ³⁰ "Go to the village ahead of you. As soon as you get there, you will find a donkey's colt tied up. No-one has ever ridden it. Untie it and bring it here. ³¹ Someone may ask you, 'Why are you untying it?' If so, say, 'The Lord needs it.'"

³² Those who were sent ahead went and found the young donkey. It was there just as Jesus had told them. ³³ They were untying the colt when its owners came. The owners asked them, "Why are you untying the colt?"

³⁴ They replied, "The Lord needs it."

³⁵ Then the disciples brought the colt to Jesus. They threw their coats on the young donkey and put Jesus on it. ³⁶ As he went along, people spread their coats on the road.

³⁷ Jesus came near the place where the road goes down the Mount of Olives. There the whole crowd of disciples began to praise God with joy. In loud voices they praised him for all the miracles they had seen. They shouted,

³⁸ "Blessed is the king who comes in the name of the Lord!"
      (Psalm 118:26)

"May there be peace and glory in the highest heaven!"

³⁹ Some of the Pharisees in the crowd spoke to Jesus. "Teacher," they said, "tell your disciples to stop!"

⁴⁰ "I tell you," he replied, "if they keep quiet, the stones will cry out."

⁴¹ He approached Jerusalem. When he saw the city, he began to weep. ⁴² He said, "I wish you had known today what would bring you peace! But now it is hidden from your eyes. ⁴³ The days will come when your enemies will arrive. They will build a wall of dirt up against your city. They will surround you and close you in on every side. ⁴⁴ You didn't recognise the time when God came

to you. So your enemies will smash you to the ground. They will destroy you and all the people inside your walls. They will not leave one stone on top of another."

Jesus Clears Out the Temple

⁴⁵ Then Jesus entered the temple courtyard. He began to drive out those who were selling there. ⁴⁶ He told them, "It is written that the Lord said, 'My house will be a house where people can pray.' *(Isaiah 56:7)* But you have made it a 'den for robbers.'" *(Jeremiah 7:11)*

⁴⁷ Every day Jesus was teaching at the temple. But the chief priests and the teachers of the law were trying to kill him. So were the leaders among the people. ⁴⁸ But they couldn't find any way to do it. All the people were paying close attention to his words.

The Authority of Jesus Is Questioned

20 One day Jesus was teaching the people in the temple courtyard. He was announcing the good news to them. The chief priests and the teachers of the law came up to him. The elders came with them. ² "Tell us by what authority you are doing these things," they all said. "Who gave you this authority?"

³ Jesus replied, "I will also ask you a question. Tell me, ⁴ was John's baptism from heaven? Or did it come from people?"

⁵ They talked to one another about it. They said, "If we say, 'From heaven', he will ask, 'Why didn't you believe him?' ⁶ But if we say, 'From people', all the people will throw stones at us and kill us. They believe that John was a prophet."

⁷ So they answered Jesus, "We don't know where John's baptism came from."

⁸ Jesus said, "Then I won't tell you by what authority I am doing these things either."

The Story of the Renters

⁹ Jesus went on to tell the people a story. "A man planted a vineyard," he said. "He rented it out to some farmers. Then he went away for a long time. ¹⁰ At harvest time he sent a slave to the renters. They were supposed to give him some of the fruit of

the vineyard. But the renters beat the slave. Then they sent him away with nothing. [11] So the man sent another slave. They beat that one and treated him badly. They also sent him away with nothing. [12] The man sent a third slave. The renters wounded him and threw him out.

[13] "Then the owner of the vineyard said, 'What should I do? I have a son, and I love him. I will send him. Maybe they will respect him.'

[14] "But when the renters saw the son, they talked the matter over. 'This is the one who will receive all the owner's property someday,' they said. 'Let's kill him. Then everything will be ours.' [15] So they threw him out of the vineyard. And they killed him.

"What will the owner of the vineyard do to the renters? [16] He will come and kill them. He will give the vineyard to others."

When the people heard this, they said, "We hope this never happens!"

[17] Jesus looked right at them and said, "Here is something I want you to explain the meaning of. It is written,

" 'The stone the builders didn't accept
    has become the most important stone of all.'   *(Psalm 118:22)*

[18] Everyone who falls on that stone will be broken to pieces. But the stone will crush anyone it falls on."

[19] The teachers of the law and the chief priests looked for a way to arrest Jesus at once. They knew he had told that story against them. But they were afraid of the people.

Is It Right to Pay the Royal Tax to Caesar?

[20] The religious leaders sent spies to keep a close watch on Jesus. The spies pretended to be sincere. They hoped they could trap Jesus with something he would say. Then they could hand him over to the power and authority of the governor. [21] So the spies questioned Jesus. "Teacher," they said, "we know that you speak and teach what is right. We know you don't favour one person over another. You teach the way of God truthfully. [22] Is it right for us to pay taxes to Caesar or not?"

[23] Jesus saw they were trying to trick him. So he said to them, [24] "Show me a silver coin. Whose picture and words are on it?"

"Caesar's," they replied.

[25] He said to them, "Then give back to Caesar what belongs to Caesar. And give back to God what belongs to God."

[26] They were not able to trap him with what he had said there in front of all the people. Amazed by his answer, they became silent.

Marriage When the Dead Rise

[27] The Sadducees do not believe that people rise from the dead. Some of them came to Jesus with a question. [28] "Teacher," they said, "Moses wrote for us about a man's brother who dies. Suppose the brother leaves a wife but has no children. Then the man must marry the widow. He must provide children to carry on his dead brother's name. [29] There were seven brothers. The first one married a woman. He died without leaving any children. [30] The second one married her. [31] And then the third one married her. One after another, the seven brothers married her. They all died. None left any children. [32] Finally, the woman died too. [33] Now then, when the dead rise, whose wife will she be? All seven brothers were married to her."

[34] Jesus replied, "People in this world get married. And their parents give them to be married. [35] But it will not be like that when the dead rise. Those who are considered worthy to take part in the world to come won't get married. And their parents won't give them to be married. [36] They can't die anymore. They are like the angels. They are God's children. They will be given a new form of life when the dead rise. [37] Remember the story of Moses and the burning bush. Even Moses showed that the dead rise. The Lord said to him, 'I am the God of Abraham. I am the God of Isaac. And I am the God of Jacob.' *(Exodus 3:6)* [38] He is not the God of the dead. He is the God of the living. In his eyes, everyone is alive."

[39] Some of the teachers of the law replied, "You have spoken well, teacher!" [40] And no-one dared to ask him any more questions.

Whose Son Is the Messiah?

[41] Jesus said to them, "Why do people say that the Messiah is the son of David? [42] David himself says in the Book of Psalms,

> " 'The Lord said to my Lord,
>   "Sit at my right hand
> ⁴³ until I put your enemies
>   under your control." '   *(Psalm 110:1)*

⁴⁴ David calls him 'Lord'. So how can he be David's son?"

Warning Against the Teachers of the Law

⁴⁵ All the people were listening. Jesus said to his disciples,
⁴⁶ "Watch out for the teachers of the law. They like to walk
around in long robes. They love to be greeted with respect in
the market. They love to have the most important seats in the
synagogues. They also love to have the places of honour at
banquets. ⁴⁷ They take over the houses of widows. They say long
prayers to show off. God will punish these men very much."

The Widow's Offering

21 As Jesus looked up, he saw rich people putting their gifts
into the temple offering boxes. ² He also saw a poor widow
put in two very small copper coins. ³ "What I'm about to tell you
is true," Jesus said. "That poor widow has put in more than all
the others. ⁴ All these other people gave a lot because they are
rich. But even though she is poor, she put in everything. She had
nothing left to live on."

When the Temple Will Be Destroyed and the Signs of the End

⁵ Some of Jesus' disciples were talking about the temple. They
spoke about how it was decorated with beautiful stones and
with gifts that honoured God. But Jesus asked, ⁶ "Do you see all
this? The time will come when not one stone will be left on top
of another. Every stone will be thrown down."

⁷ "Teacher," they asked, "when will these things happen? And
what will be the sign that they are about to take place?"

⁸ Jesus replied, "Keep watch! Be careful that you are not
fooled. Many will come in my name. They will claim, 'I am he!'
And they will say, 'The time is near!' Do not follow them. ⁹ Do not
be afraid when you hear about wars and about fighting against

rulers. Those things must happen first. But the end will not come right away."

¹⁰ Then Jesus said to them, "Nation will fight against nation. Kingdom will fight against kingdom. ¹¹ In many places there will be powerful earthquakes. People will go hungry. There will be terrible diseases. Things will happen that will make people afraid. There will be great and miraculous signs from heaven.

¹² "But before all this, people will arrest you and treat you badly. They will hand you over to synagogues and put you in prison. You will be brought to kings and governors. All this will happen to you because of my name. ¹³ And so you will be witnesses about me. ¹⁴ But make up your mind not to worry in advance about how to stand up for yourselves. ¹⁵ I will give you words of wisdom. None of your enemies will be able to withstand them or prove them wrong. ¹⁶ Even your parents, brothers, sisters, relatives and friends will hand you over to the authorities. The authorities will put some of you to death. ¹⁷ Everyone will hate you because of me. ¹⁸ But not a hair on your head will be harmed. ¹⁹ Remain strong in the faith, and you will receive eternal life.

²⁰ "A time is coming when you will see armies surround Jerusalem. Then you will know that it will soon be destroyed. ²¹ Those who are in Judea should then escape to the mountains. Those in the city should get out. Those in the country should not enter the city. ²² This is the time when God will punish Jerusalem. Everything will come true, just as it has been written. ²³ How awful it will be in those days for pregnant women! How awful for nursing mothers! There will be terrible suffering in the land. There will be great anger against those people. ²⁴ Some will be killed by the sword. Others will be taken as prisoners to all the nations. Jerusalem will be taken over by Gentiles until the times of the Gentiles come to an end.

²⁵ "There will be signs in the sun, moon and stars. The nations of the earth will be in terrible pain. They will be puzzled by the roaring and tossing of the sea. ²⁶ Terror will make people faint. They will be worried about what is happening in the world. The sun, moon and stars will be shaken from their places. ²⁷ At that time people will see the Son of Man coming in a cloud. He will

come with power and great glory. ²⁸ When these things begin to take place, stand up. Hold your head up with joy and hope. The time when you will be set free will be very close."

²⁹ Jesus told them a story. "Look at the fig tree and all the trees," he said. ³⁰ "When you see leaves appear on the branches, you know that summer is near. ³¹ In the same way, when you see these things happening, you will know that God's kingdom is near.

³² "What I'm about to tell you is true. The people living now will certainly not pass away until all these things have happened. ³³ Heaven and earth will pass away. But my words will never pass away.

³⁴ "Be careful. If you aren't, your hearts will be loaded down with wasteful living, drunkenness and the worries of life. Then the day the Son of Man returns will close on you like a trap. It will happen suddenly. ³⁵ That day will come on every person who lives on the whole earth. ³⁶ Always keep watching. Pray that you will be able to escape all that is about to happen. Also, pray that you will not be judged guilty when the Son of Man comes."

³⁷ Each day Jesus taught at the temple. And each evening he went to spend the night on the hill called the Mount of Olives. ³⁸ All the people came to the temple early in the morning. They wanted to hear Jesus speak.

Judas Agrees to Hand Jesus Over

22 The Feast of Unleavened Bread, called the Passover, was near. ² The chief priests and the teachers of the law were looking for a way to get rid of Jesus. They were afraid of the people. ³ Then Satan entered Judas, who was called Iscariot. Judas was one of the 12 disciples. ⁴ He went to the chief priests and the officers of the temple guard. He talked with them about how he could hand Jesus over to them. ⁵ They were delighted and agreed to give him money. ⁶ Judas accepted their offer. He watched for the right time to hand Jesus over to them. He wanted to do it when no crowd was around.

The Last Supper

⁷ Then the day of Unleavened Bread came. That was the time the Passover lamb had to be sacrificed. ⁸ Jesus sent Peter and

John on ahead. "Go," he told them. "Prepare for us to eat the Passover meal."

⁹ "Where do you want us to prepare for it?" they asked.

¹⁰ Jesus replied, "When you enter the city, a man carrying a jar of water will meet you. Follow him to the house he enters. ¹¹ Then say to the owner of the house, 'The Teacher asks, "Where is the guest room? Where can I eat the Passover meal with my disciples?" ' ¹² He will show you a large upstairs room with furniture already in it. Prepare for us to eat there."

¹³ Peter and John left. They found things just as Jesus had told them. So they prepared the Passover meal.

¹⁴ When the hour came, Jesus and his apostles took their places at the table. ¹⁵ He said to them, "I have really looked forward to eating this Passover meal with you. I wanted to do this before I suffer. ¹⁶ I tell you, I will not eat the Passover meal again until it is celebrated in God's kingdom."

¹⁷ After Jesus took the cup, he gave thanks. He said, "Take this cup and share it among yourselves. ¹⁸ I tell you, I will not drink wine with you again until God's kingdom comes."

¹⁹ Then Jesus took bread. He gave thanks and broke it. He handed it to them and said, "This is my body. It is given for you. Every time you eat it, do this in memory of me."

²⁰ In the same way, after the supper he took the cup. He said, "This cup is the new covenant in my blood. It is poured out for you. ²¹ But someone here is going to hand me over to my enemies. His hand is with mine on the table. ²² The Son of Man will go to his death, just as God has already decided. But how terrible it will be for the one who hands him over!" ²³ The apostles began to ask one another about this. They wondered which one of them would do it.

²⁴ They also started to argue. They disagreed about which of them was thought to be the most important person. ²⁵ Jesus said to them, "The kings of the Gentiles hold power over their people. And those who order them around call themselves Protectors. ²⁶ But you must not be like that. Instead, the most important among you should be like the youngest. The one who rules should be like the one who serves. ²⁷ Who is more important? Is it the one at the table, or the one who serves? Isn't it the one

who is at the table? But I am among you as one who serves. ²⁸ You have stood by me during my troubles. ²⁹ And I give you a kingdom, just as my Father gave me a kingdom. ³⁰ Then you will eat and drink at my table in my kingdom. And you will sit on thrones, judging the 12 tribes of Israel.

³¹ "Simon, Simon! Satan has asked to sift all of you disciples like wheat. ³² But I have prayed for you, Simon. I have prayed that your faith will not fail. When you have turned back, help your brothers to be strong."

³³ But Simon replied, "Lord, I am ready to go with you to prison and to death."

³⁴ Jesus answered, "I tell you, Peter, you will say three times that you don't know me. And you will do it before the cock crows today."

³⁵ Then Jesus asked the disciples, "Did you need anything when I sent you without a purse, bag or sandals?"

"Nothing," they answered.

³⁶ He said to them, "But now if you have a purse, take it. And also take a bag. If you don't have a sword, sell your coat and buy one. ³⁷ It is written, 'He was counted among those who had committed crimes.' *(Isaiah 53:12)* I tell you that what is written about me must come true. Yes, it is already coming true."

³⁸ The disciples said, "See, Lord, here are two swords."

"Two swords are enough!" he replied.

Jesus Prays on the Mount of Olives

³⁹ Jesus went out as usual to the Mount of Olives. His disciples followed him. ⁴⁰ When they reached the place, Jesus spoke. "Pray that you won't fall into sin when you are tempted," he said to them. ⁴¹ Then he went a short distance away from them. There he got down on his knees and prayed. ⁴² He said, "Father, if you are willing, take this cup of suffering away from me. But do what you want, not what I want." ⁴³ An angel from heaven appeared to Jesus and gave him strength. ⁴⁴ Because he was very sad and troubled, he prayed even harder. His sweat was like drops of blood falling to the ground.

⁴⁵ After that, he got up from prayer and went back to the

disciples. He found them sleeping. They were worn out because they were very sad. ⁴⁶ "Why are you sleeping?" he asked them. "Get up! Pray that you won't fall into sin when you are tempted."

Jesus Is Arrested

⁴⁷ While Jesus was still speaking, a crowd came up. The man named Judas was leading them. He was one of the 12 disciples. Judas approached Jesus to kiss him. ⁴⁸ But Jesus asked him, "Judas, are you handing over the Son of Man with a kiss?"

⁴⁹ Jesus' followers saw what was going to happen. So they said, "Lord, should we use our swords against them?" ⁵⁰ One of them struck the slave of the high priest and cut off his right ear.

⁵¹ But Jesus answered, "Stop this!" And he touched the man's ear and healed him.

⁵² Then Jesus spoke to the chief priests, the officers of the temple guard, and the elders. They had all come for him. "Am I leading a band of armed men against you?" he asked. "Do you have to come with swords and clubs? ⁵³ Every day I was with you in the temple courtyard. And you didn't lay a hand on me. But this is your hour. This is when darkness rules."

Peter Says He Does Not Know Jesus

⁵⁴ Then the men arrested Jesus and led him away. They took him into the high priest's house. Peter followed from far away. ⁵⁵ Some people there started a fire in the middle of the courtyard. Then they sat down together. Peter sat down with them. ⁵⁶ A female servant saw him sitting there in the firelight. She looked closely at him. Then she said, "This man was with Jesus."

⁵⁷ But Peter said he had not been with him. "Woman, I don't know him," he said.

⁵⁸ A little later someone else saw Peter. "You also are one of them," he said.

"No," Peter replied. "I'm not!"

⁵⁹ About an hour later, another person spoke up. "This fellow must have been with Jesus," he said. "He is from Galilee."

⁶⁰ Peter replied, "Man, I don't know what you're talking about!" Just as he was speaking, the cock crowed. ⁶¹ The Lord turned and looked right at Peter. Then Peter remembered what the Lord

had spoken to him. "The cock will crow today," Jesus had said. "Before it does, you will say three times that you don't know me." [62] Peter went outside. He broke down and cried.

The Guards Make Fun of Jesus

[63] There were men guarding Jesus. They began laughing at him and beating him. [64] They blindfolded him. They said, "Prophesy! Who hit you?" [65] They also said many other things to make fun of him.

Jesus Is Brought to Pilate and Herod

[66] At dawn the elders of the people met together. These included the chief priests and the teachers of the law. Jesus was led to them. [67] "If you are the Messiah," they said, "tell us."

Jesus answered, "If I tell you, you will not believe me. [68] And if I asked you, you would not answer. [69] But from now on, the Son of Man will be seated at the right hand of the mighty God."

[70] They all asked, "Are you the Son of God then?"

He replied, "You say that I am."

[71] Then they said, "Why do we need any more witnesses? We have heard it from his own lips."

23 Then the whole group got up and led Jesus off to Pilate. [2] They began to bring charges against Jesus. They said, "We have found this man misleading our people. He is against paying taxes to Caesar. And he claims to be Messiah, a king."

[3] So Pilate asked Jesus, "Are you the king of the Jews?"

"You have said so," Jesus replied.

[4] Then Pilate spoke to the chief priests and the crowd. He announced, "I find no basis for a charge against this man."

[5] But they kept it up. They said, "His teaching stirs up the people all over Judea. He started in Galilee and has come all the way here."

[6] When Pilate heard this, he asked if the man was from Galilee. [7] He learned that Jesus was from Herod's area of authority. So Pilate sent Jesus to Herod. At that time Herod was also in Jerusalem.

[8] When Herod saw Jesus, he was very pleased. He had been

wanting to see Jesus for a long time. He had heard much about him. He hoped to see Jesus perform a sign of some kind. ⁹ Herod asked him many questions, but Jesus gave him no answer. ¹⁰ The chief priests and the teachers of the law were standing there. With loud shouts they brought charges against him. ¹¹ Herod and his soldiers laughed at him and made fun of him. They dressed him in a beautiful robe. Then they sent him back to Pilate. ¹² That day Herod and Pilate became friends. Before this time they had been enemies.

¹³ Pilate called together the chief priests, the rulers and the people. ¹⁴ He said to them, "You brought me this man. You said he was turning the people against the authorities. I have questioned him in front of you. I have found no basis for your charges against him. ¹⁵ Herod hasn't either. So he sent Jesus back to us. As you can see, Jesus has done nothing that is worthy of death. ¹⁶⁻¹⁷ So I will just have him whipped and let him go."

¹⁸ But the whole crowd shouted, "Kill this man! But let Barabbas go!" ¹⁹ Barabbas had been thrown into prison. He had taken part in a struggle in the city against the authorities. He had also committed murder.

²⁰ Pilate wanted to let Jesus go. So he made an appeal to the crowd again. ²¹ But they kept shouting, "Crucify him! Crucify him!"

²² Pilate spoke to them for the third time. "Why?" he asked. "What wrong has this man done? I have found no reason to have him put to death. So I will just have him whipped and let him go."

²³ But with loud shouts they kept calling for Jesus to be crucified. The people's shouts won out. ²⁴ So Pilate decided to give them what they wanted. ²⁵ He set free the man they asked for. The man had been thrown in prison for murder and for fighting against the authorities. Pilate handed Jesus over to them so they could carry out their plans.

Jesus Is Nailed to a Cross

²⁶ As the soldiers led Jesus away, they took hold of Simon. Simon was from Cyrene. He was on his way in from the country. They put a wooden cross on his shoulders. Then they made him carry it behind Jesus. ²⁷ A large number of people followed Jesus. Some were women whose hearts were filled with sorrow.

They cried loudly because of him. ²⁸ Jesus turned and said to them, "Daughters of Jerusalem, do not weep for me. Weep for yourselves and for your children. ²⁹ The time will come when you will say, 'Blessed are the women who can't have children! Blessed are those who never gave birth or fed babies!' ³⁰ It is written,

> " 'The people will say to the mountains, "Fall on us!"
>   They'll say to the hills, "Cover us!" ' '   *(Hosea 10:8)*

³¹ People do these things when trees are green. So what will happen when trees are dry?"

³² Two other men were also led out with Jesus to be killed. Both of them had broken the law. ³³ The soldiers brought them to the place called the Skull. There they nailed Jesus to the cross. He hung between the two criminals. One was on his right and one was on his left. ³⁴ Jesus said, "Father, forgive them. They don't know what they are doing." The soldiers divided up his clothes by casting lots.

³⁵ The people stood there watching. The rulers even made fun of Jesus. They said, "He saved others. Let him save himself if he is God's Messiah, the Chosen One."

³⁶ The soldiers also came up and poked fun at him. They offered him wine vinegar. ³⁷ They said, "If you are the king of the Jews, save yourself."

³⁸ A written sign had been placed above him. It read,

THIS IS THE KING OF THE JEWS.

³⁹ One of the criminals hanging there made fun of Jesus. He said, "Aren't you the Messiah? Save yourself! Save us!"

⁴⁰ But the other criminal scolded him. "Don't you have any respect for God?" he said. "Remember, you are under the same sentence of death. ⁴¹ We are being punished fairly. We are getting just what our actions call for. But this man hasn't done anything wrong."

⁴² Then he said, "Jesus, remember me when you come into your kingdom."

⁴³ Jesus answered him, "What I'm about to tell you is true. Today you will be with me in paradise."

Jesus Dies

⁴⁴ It was now about noon. Then darkness covered the whole land until three o'clock. ⁴⁵ The sun had stopped shining. The temple curtain was torn in two. ⁴⁶ Jesus called out in a loud voice, "Father, into your hands I commit my life." After he said this, he took his last breath.

⁴⁷ The Roman commander saw what had happened. He praised God and said, "Jesus was surely a man who did what was right." ⁴⁸ The people had gathered to watch this sight. When they saw what happened, they felt very sad. Then they went away. ⁴⁹ But all those who knew Jesus stood not very far away, watching these things. They included the women who had followed him from Galilee.

Jesus Is Buried

⁵⁰ A man named Joseph was a member of the Jewish Council. He was a good and honest man. ⁵¹ Joseph had not agreed with what the leaders had decided and done. He was from Arimathea, a town in Judea. He himself was waiting for God's kingdom. ⁵² Joseph went to Pilate and asked for Jesus' body. ⁵³ Joseph took it down and wrapped it in linen cloth. Then he placed it in a tomb cut in the rock. No-one had ever been buried there. ⁵⁴ It was Preparation Day. The Sabbath day was about to begin.

⁵⁵ The women who had come with Jesus from Galilee followed Joseph. They saw the tomb and how Jesus' body was placed in it. ⁵⁶ Then they went home. There they prepared spices and perfumes. But they rested on the Sabbath day in order to obey the Law.

Jesus Rises from the Dead

24 It was very early in the morning on the first day of the week. The women took the spices they had prepared. Then they went to the tomb. ² They found the stone rolled away from it. ³ When they entered the tomb, they did not find the body of the Lord Jesus. ⁴ They were wondering about this. Suddenly two men in clothes as bright as lightning stood beside them. ⁵ The women were terrified. They bowed down with their

faces to the ground. Then the men said to them, "Why do you look for the living among the dead? ⁶ Jesus is not here! He has risen! Remember how he told you he would rise. It was while he was still with you in Galilee. ⁷ He said, 'The Son of Man must be handed over to sinful people. He must be nailed to a cross. On the third day he will rise from the dead.' " ⁸ Then the women remembered Jesus' words.

⁹ They came back from the tomb. They told all these things to the 11 apostles and to all the others. ¹⁰ Mary Magdalene, Joanna, Mary the mother of James, and the others with them were the ones who told the apostles. ¹¹ But the apostles did not believe the women. Their words didn't make any sense to them. ¹² But Peter got up and ran to the tomb. He bent over and saw the strips of linen lying by themselves. Then he went away, wondering what had happened.

On the Road to Emmaus

¹³ That same day two of Jesus' followers were going to a village called Emmaus. It was about seven miles from Jerusalem. ¹⁴ They were talking with each other about everything that had happened. ¹⁵ As they talked about those things, Jesus himself came up and walked along with them. ¹⁶ But God kept them from recognising him.

¹⁷ Jesus asked them, "What are you talking about as you walk along?"

They stood still, and their faces were sad. ¹⁸ One of them was named Cleopas. He said to Jesus, "Are you the only person visiting Jerusalem who doesn't know? Don't you know about the things that have happened there in the last few days?"

¹⁹ "What things?" Jesus asked.

"About Jesus of Nazareth," they replied. "He was a prophet. He was powerful in what he said and did in the sight of God and all the people. ²⁰ The chief priests and our rulers handed Jesus over to be sentenced to death. They nailed him to a cross. ²¹ But we had hoped that he was the one who was going to set Israel free. Also, it is the third day since all this happened. ²² Some of our women amazed us too. Early this morning they went to the tomb. ²³ But they didn't find his body. So they came and told us what they had seen. They saw angels, who said Jesus was alive. [24] Then some of our friends went to the tomb. They saw it was empty, just as the women had said. They didn't see Jesus' body there."

[25] Jesus said to them, "How foolish you are! How long it takes you to believe all that the prophets said! [26] Didn't the Messiah have to suffer these things and then receive his glory?" [27] Jesus explained to them what was said about himself in all the Scriptures. He began with Moses and all the Prophets.

[28] They approached the village where they were going. Jesus kept walking as if he were going further. [29] But they tried hard to keep him from leaving. They said, "Stay with us. It is nearly evening. The day is almost over." So he went in to stay with them.

[30] He joined them at the table. Then he took bread and gave thanks. He broke it and began to give it to them. [31] Their eyes were opened, and they recognised him. But then he disappeared from their sight. [32] They said to each other, "He explained to us what the Scriptures meant. Weren't we excited as he talked with us on the road?"

[33] They got up and returned at once to Jerusalem. There they found the 11 disciples and those with them. They were all gathered together. [34] They were saying, "It's true! The Lord has risen! He has appeared to Simon!" [35] Then the two of them told what had happened to them on the way. They told how they had recognised Jesus when he broke the bread.

Jesus Appears to the Disciples

[36] The disciples were still talking about this when Jesus himself suddenly stood among them. He said, "May you have peace!"

[37] They were surprised and terrified. They thought they were seeing a ghost. [38] Jesus said to them, "Why are you troubled? Why do you have doubts in your minds? [39] Look at my hands and my feet. It's really me! Touch me and see. A ghost does not have a body or bones. But you can see that I do."

[40] After he said that, he showed them his hands and feet. [41] But they still did not believe it. They were amazed and filled with joy. So Jesus asked them, "Do you have anything here to eat?"

[42] They gave him a piece of cooked fish. [43] He took it and ate it in front of them.

[44] Jesus said to them, "This is what I told you while I was still with you. Everything written about me in the Law of Moses, the Prophets and the Psalms must come true."

[45] Then he opened their minds so they could understand the Scriptures. [46] He told them, "This is what is written. The Messiah will suffer. He will rise from the dead on the third day. [47] His followers will preach in his name. They will tell others to turn away from their sins and be forgiven. People from every nation will hear it, beginning at Jerusalem. [48] You have seen these things with your own eyes. [49] I am going to send you what my Father has promised. But for now, stay in the city. Stay there until you have received power from heaven."

Jesus Is Taken Up into Heaven

[50] Jesus led his disciples out to the area near Bethany. Then he lifted up his hands and blessed them. [51] While he was blessing them, he left them. He was taken up into heaven. [52] Then they worshipped him. With great joy, they returned to Jerusalem. [53] Every day they went to the temple, praising God.

THE CHURCH
OF ENGLAND

To find out more about Jesus you could visit a
local church or contact us at Lambeth Palace
talkaboutjesus@lambethpalace.org